101 KEY IDEAS

Linguistics

101 KEY IDEAS

Linguistics

Richard Horsey

TEACH YOURSELF BOOKS

For UK order queries: please contact Bookpoint Ltd, 78 Milton Park, Abingdon, Oxon OX14 4TD. Telephone: (44) 01235 400414, Fax: (44) 01235 400454. Lines are open from 9.00–6.00, Monday to Saturday, with a 24 hour message answering service. Email address: orders@bookpoint.co.uk

For U.S.A. & Canada order queries: please contact NTC/Contemporary Publishing, 4255 West Touhy Avenue, Lincolnwood, Illinois 60646–1975, U.S.A. Telephone: (847) 679 5500, Fax: (847) 679 2494.

Long renowned as the authoritative source for self-guided learning – with more than 30 million copies sold worldwide – the *Teach Yourself* series includes over 200 titles in the fields of languages, crafts, hobbies, business and education.

British Library Cataloguing in Publication Data
A catalogue record for this title is available from The British Library.

Library of Congress Catalog Card Number: On file

First published in UK 2001 by Hodder Headline Plc, 338 Euston Road, London, NW1 3BH.

First published in US 2001 by NTC/Contemporary Publishing, 4255 West Touhy Avenue, Lincolnwood (Chicago), Illinois 60646–1975 USA.

The 'Teach Yourself' name and logo are registered trade marks of Hodder & Stoughton Ltd.

Copyright © 2001 Richard Horsey

Cover photo from Mike Stones.

Typeset by Transet Limited, Coventry, England.
Printed in Great Britain for Hodder & Stoughton Educational, a division of Hodder Headline Plc, 338 Euston Road, London NW1 3BH by Cox & Wyman Ltd, Reading, Berkshire.

Impression number   10 9 8 7 6 5 4 3 2 1
Year   2005 2004 2003 2002 2001

Contents

Introduction

Welcome to the **Teach Yourself 101 Key Ideas** series. We hope that you will find both this book and others in the series to be useful, interesting and informative. The purpose of the series is to provide an introduction to a wide range of subjects, in a way that is entertaining and easy to absorb.

Each book contains 101 short accounts of key ideas or terms which are regarded as central to that subject. The accounts are presented in alphabetical order for ease of reference. All of the books in the series are written in order to be meaningful whether or not you have previous knowledge of the subject. They will be useful to you whether you are a general reader, are on a pre-university course, or have just started at university.

We have designed the series to be a combination of a text book and a dictionary. We felt that many text books are too long for easy reference, while the entries in dictionaries are often too short to provide sufficient detail. The **Teach Yourself 101 Key Ideas** series gives the best of both worlds! Here are books that you do not have to read cover to cover, or in any set order. Dip into them when you need to know the meaning of a term, and you will find a short, but comprehensive account which will be of real help with those essays and assignments. The terms are described in a straightforward way with a careful selection of academic words thrown in for good measure!

So if you need a quick and inexpensive introduction to a subject, **Teach Yourself 101 Key Ideas** is for you. And incidentally, if you have any suggestions about this book or the series, do let us know. It would be great to hear from you.

Best wishes with your studies!

Paul Oliver
Series Editor

[**A note on conventions**: quoted expressions of English and other languages are given in italics, whereas the meanings of expressions are given in roman text enclosed in single quotes. Technical terms are also given in single quotes when they are first introduced. Bold text is reserved for highlighting relevant parts of quoted expressions. An asterisk before a sentence or other expression is used to indicate that it is ungrammatical.]

Acquisition of language

Children have a remarkable ability. Regardless of their general level of intelligence, all children (unless they have a severe mental or physical impairment) are essentially fluent in their native language by about age six. They seem to achieve this effortlessly and without any systematic teaching. Children can even learn two or more native languages at the same time. How do they do this? And why is it so much more difficult to learn a language later in life?

Linguists and psychologists studying these questions have discovered some interesting things. First, children are not taught language: parents sometimes try to 'teach' language to their children, but this is not systematic and has been shown to have little influence. In some cultures, parents do not even talk to their children until they can talk back, but the children still acquire language at about the same speed. Second, children seem to know things that they could not have learned from the language they have heard. For example, children are able to produce grammatical sentences of a kind they have never encountered before. Third, children are not generally corrected when they make grammatical mistakes – studies have shown that parents tend to be much more concerned with truthfulness and politeness.

These facts suggest strongly that children are genetically endowed with much of what they need to know to learn language – they have what can be called a 'language acquisition device'. This device gradually 'switches off' as children grow older, and by puberty it is no longer functioning. This is why it is so difficult for older children and adults to learn a language – and why it was so hard to learn all those French verb endings at school!

> ### see also...
> *Bilingualism; Motherese; Psycholinguistics*

Adjective

Words such as *happy* and *interesting*, which modify nouns, are members of the class of adjectives. In English, adjectives occur before the noun they modify (as in *a **happy** person*), after certain verbs (as in *the person is **happy***), and may be modified by *very* (as in *a very **happy** person*). Adjectives may also be used in a comparative form (e.g. *happier* or *more interesting*) and a superlative form (e.g. *happiest* or *most interesting*).

Adjectives also have certain morphological properties. They can take the prefix *un-* or *in-* to form a new adjective with opposite meaning (e.g. *unhappy*) and many can take the suffix *-ness* or *-ity* to form a noun (e.g. *happiness*). In some languages, adjectives agree with the nouns they modify. For example, in French we find ***petit** garçon* 'little boy' but ***petite** maison* 'little house'. Because *maison* is grammatically feminine in French, the adjective modifying it must be marked as feminine (by adding an *-e*).

Adverbs have similar properties to adjectives (for example, both can be modified by *very*, and both take the prefix *un-* or *in-*), and therefore some linguists classify adverbs as a special kind of adjective.

English has many adjectives, but some languages have few or none at all. In these languages, verbs or nouns are used to express adjectival meanings.

see also...

Adverb and adverbial; Agreement; Morphology; Part of speech

Adjunct

Some elements of a phrase or clause are required by the grammar, while others are optional. For example, in the sentence *'Teresa sliced the bread yesterday'*, the adverb *yesterday* is optional, whereas *the bread* is not optional – we can say *'Teresa sliced the bread'* but not **'Teresa sliced yesterday'*. These optional elements are known as 'adjuncts'.

Adjuncts may express different kinds of information, such as time (as in the previous example), manner (as in *'Peter speaks **too quickly'*), place (as in *'He always has dinner **at this restaurant'*), instrument (as in *'Peter polished his car **with an old cloth'*) and purpose (as in *'John is going to the station **to catch a train'*). Adjuncts are typically, but not always, adverb phrases (such as *yesterday* or *too quickly*) or preposition phrases (such as *at this restaurant* or *with an old cloth*).

It is not possible, however, to tell whether something is an adjunct just by looking at what type of information it expresses or what kind of phrase it is. In the sentence *'Peter is in the garden'*, the preposition phrase *in the garden* expresses information about place, but it cannot be omitted, and it is therefore a complement rather than an adjunct. The same phrase in the sentence *'Peter plays the guitar in the garden'* is optional, however, and so in this sentence it is an adjunct.

see also...

Complement; Constituent; Phrase

Adverb and adverbial

Words such as *happily* and *often*, which most commonly express the mode of action of a verb, are members of the class of adverbs. In English, many adverbs are derived from adjectives by suffixing *-ly*.

Like adjectives, adverbs can be modified by *very* (e.g. *very **often***) and in many cases can take the prefix *-un* or *-in* (e.g. *unhappily*). For these and other reasons, some linguists prefer to regard adverbs as a special kind of adjective.

As well as modifying verbs, adverbs also modify adjectives (e.g. ***particularly*** *good*), other adverbs (e.g. ***particularly*** *calmly*) and sometimes whole sentences (e.g. ***fortunately***, *no one was injured*). Adverbs are often classified according to whether they indicate manner, time or place.

In traditional grammars and some dictionaries, the term 'adverb' is applied to any word that does not appear to fit into any of the other word classes. For example, *quickly, not, yesterday, very* and *when* have all been classified as adverbs, although they have very few grammatical properties in common. While it is true that they may appear to modify time, manner and so on, the same is true of many kinds of phrase (e.g. *on Monday, next week, when the time comes*). For this reason, linguists now tend to be rather strict in assigning words to the class of adverbs. The term 'adverbial' is then used for words and phrases that modify in the same way as adverbs.

see also...

Adjective; Part of speech; Phrase

Agent and patient

Verbs usually express actions or states of affairs, and these actions or states of affairs typically involve one or more participants. For example, the verb *sleep* involves one participant, the person who sleeps. The verb *kick* involves two participants, the kicker and the thing that is kicked.

There are two ways of classifying expressions referring to such participants. It is possible to classify them on the basis of their grammatical function – that is, as subjects, direct objects, indirect objects and so on. For example, in the sentence *'John sleeps'* we can identify *John* as the subject. It is also possible to classify participants in terms of their role in the action or state of affairs described by the verb (what is known as their 'semantic role' or 'thematic role'). For example, in the sentence *'The boy kicked the ball'*, we say that *the boy* is the 'agent' (since it is the boy who does the kicking) and *the ball* is the 'patient' (since it is the ball that has something done to it). Other thematic roles include 'instrument', 'recipient' and 'goal'.

There is clearly some relation between what thematic role an expression has and its grammatical function. For example, subjects are typically agents, direct objects are typically patients, and indirect objects are typically recipients or goals. There are many exceptions, however (e.g. *the ball* is the subject of *'The ball rolled down the hill'*, but it is not the agent). It has proved very difficult to develop a set of thematic roles that can be consistently applied and precisely defined.

see also...

Argument; Object; Subject

Agreement

Have you ever wondered why in English we say *'I walk'* but *'He walks'*, and why in French one says *petit garçon* 'small boy', but *petite maison* 'small house'? The reason is that these languages (along with many others) have what is known as 'agreement' (sometimes also called 'concord'). In these languages, certain words change their endings to 'agree with' other words in the sentence. For example, French adjectives such as *petit* take a feminine *-e* ending when the noun they modify is grammatically feminine (as *maison* is). Similarly, English verbs like *walk* take an *-s* ending when their subject is third-person singular (e.g. *he* or *Sarah*).

Agreement is very common in the world's languages, but the extent of agreement varies widely. English, for example, has little need for agreement, because its word order is relatively fixed, and so it is easy to tell which words 'go together' (we know that *small* and *house* go together in *'Piglet lives in a small house'* because of their order in the sentence). Some languages, such as Chinese, have no agreement at all. Latin, by way of contrast, has free word order and without agreement it would be very difficult to tell which words went together. For example, in Latin the sentence *'Piglet lives in a small house'* could have the word order 'in-a-house-small-Piglet-lives' and without agreement it would be impossible to know whether *small* modified *house* or *Piglet*. (The agreement that remains in English is mostly a relic from a time when English had free word order like Latin.)

see also...

Morphology

6

Ambiguity

ewspaper headlines such as *'Iraqi head seeks arms'* are amusing because they have two possible interpretations, one of which was probably not intended (or even noticed) by the writer. When a word or phrase has more than one interpretation, it is said to be 'ambiguous'. The ways in which we deal with ambiguity provide valuable evidence for theories of grammar and theories of language processing.

There are a number of different sources of ambiguity. Perhaps the most obvious is when a word has more than one meaning ('homonymy'), as with *head* and *arms* in the above example. This is known as 'lexical ambiguity'. In other cases, a sentence may be ambiguous even though none of its words is, as in *'The blast was attributed to a build-up of gas by one town official'*. In this case, it is the structure of the sentence which is ambiguous (the phrase *by one town official* could be associated with *build-up* or *attributed*). The two meanings would be represented by two different tree diagrams. This is known as 'structural ambiguity' or 'syntactic ambiguity'.

Other kinds of ambiguity are less obvious. For example, *'Some man loves every woman'* has two possible meanings, one where there is a single man who loves all women and one where every woman is loved by at least one man (but not necessarily the same one). The syntactic structure in each case is the same, however. This is known as 'scope ambiguity'. A further kind of ambiguity is seen in the sentence *'John doesn't know if he will win'*. Here, the pronoun *he* can refer to John, or to someone else. This is known as 'referential ambiguity'.

> **see also...**
> Homonymy and polysemy; Tree diagram

Analytic and synthetic language

There are two main ways in which languages can be classified into groups. They can be classified in terms of their historical (or 'genetic') relationships. Thus English, Latin, and Russian would be classified together (along with many other languages), because they are all descended from a single ancestor. Languages can also be classified according to similarities in their structure. This is known as 'typology'. The most common typology is based on the word order of sentences, but languages can also be classified according to the internal structure of their words ('morphology').

In some languages (e.g. Latin and Arabic) words change their form to indicate grammatical properties. For example, nouns change their endings to indicate whether they are singular or plural, the subject or the object, and so on. Languages like this are known as 'synthetic' (or 'inflecting').

In other languages (e.g. Chinese), words have little or no internal structure. In these languages, words always have the same form and grammatical information is provided by the use of word order and special grammatical words (so there might be a separate word meaning 'plural', for example). These languages are known as 'analytic'. It is not always clear whether to classify a language as analytic or synthetic (English is a language that seems to have properties of both types) and many languages show these properties to different degrees.

Some linguists also recognise a third type, known as 'polysynthetic'. In these languages (e.g. Eskimo and Mohawk), words can be long and complex and can correspond to what would be an entire sentence in English. Because they appear to have a very different structure from that of other languages, they have been important in helping to provide evidence for which properties of language are universal.

see also...

Language family; Morphology; Typology; Word order

Anaphora

Consider a sentence such as *'Bill likes to drink, but he tries not to'*. On the most natural interpretation of this sentence, the pronoun *he* means *Bill*. *He* has no meaning of its own – it takes its meaning from another word in the sentence. When a pronoun takes its meaning from some other word or phrase, this is known as 'anaphora'. The word or phrase whose meaning is taken is known as the 'antecedent'.

Pronouns can also take their meaning from words outside the sentence. For example, in *'Eric had a heart attack last year. Bill likes to drink, but he tries not to'*, the pronoun *he* can take *Eric* as its antecedent. It is even possible that the antecedent has not been mentioned at all in previous discourse (as in *'Bill likes to drink, but he [pointing to George] tries not to'*).

Pronouns, then, can take their meaning from other words or phrases in the sentence, from words or phrases in preceding sentences, or from the context. There is a special type of pronoun, however, that can only take its meaning from words or phrases within the sentence. Such pronouns are known as 'anaphors'. For example, *'John pleases himself'* can only mean 'John pleases John' (not 'John pleases Eric'). And while *'John pleases her'* can mean *'John pleases Natalie'*, the sentence **'John pleases herself'* is completely ungrammatical. The rules governing the use of anaphors are complex and discovering these rules is a major focus of current linguistics.

see also...

Pronoun and proform

Animal communication

Most animals communicate with each other in some way and some of their systems of communication are quite complex. Honeybees, for example, can accurately convey to each other the direction, distance and quality of a source of nectar. Vervet monkeys have a number of distinct vocalisations, including different alarm calls for leopards, eagles, and snakes (and when recordings of these alarm calls are played to other vervet monkeys, they respond appropriately – by running up a tree, looking to the sky, or searching in the grass). How are such systems of communication different from human language?

Animal communication appears to be of two basic kinds. The calls of birds and non-human primates consist of a small number of signals, each of which has a fixed purpose (danger call, food call, distress call and so on). Bees, however, have an unlimited number of signals (they can convey any combination of distance, direction and quality), but the system cannot be used to communicate anything else. In both cases, the communication is largely predictable, with the signal occurring only in the presence of the right stimulus. Contrast this with human speech – we do not necessarily talk about eagles when we see one; conversely, we can discuss eagles even when there are none around.

In recent decades there have been many attempts to teach human language to apes. These attempts have met with mixed success. While there is some evidence that they can learn large numbers of word-like symbols, there is little evidence that apes are able to learn much syntax. Indeed, language is such a powerful tool that it would be surprising if apes had a significant linguistic ability that they failed to make use of in their natural environment.

see also...

Communication; Syntax

Argument

All verbs require a certain number of other elements to be present in the sentence. These elements required by a verb are known as 'arguments' of that verb. The arguments of a verb usually denote the participants in the activity or event described by the verb. For example, an activity such as sleeping involves only one participant (the person who sleeps), so the verb *sleep* has one argument. This argument is the subject – for example, *John* in the sentence *'**John** sleeps'*.

Other verbs have more than one argument. For example, biting involves two participants (the person or thing which does the biting and the person or thing bitten), so the verb *bite* has two arguments. These two arguments are the subject and the object – for example, *the dog* and *the cat* in the sentence *'**The dog** bit **the cat**'*. Giving involves three participants (the person who does the giving, the thing given and the person it is given to), so the verb *give* has three arguments: *'**Teresa** gave **Adam a book**'*.

Arguments are typically noun phrases, but other types of phrase can also act as arguments, as can clauses. (Some linguists prefer to use the term argument only for noun phrases, however.) As well as arguments, a sentence may, in addition, contain various optional phrases known as 'adjuncts'. For example, in the sentence *'**Teresa** gave **Adam a book** on Tuesday'*, the optional phrase *on Tuesday* is an adjunct, not an argument.

see also...

Adjunct; Complement; Verb

Aspect

Language and time are intimately connected and languages have a variety of ways of expressing temporal notions. The most obvious way is by using words that refer explicitly to time: *now, yesterday, next week, in a million years*. Many languages also express time grammatically, for example, by using tense to express whether the activity denoted by the verb occurred in the past, present or future. As well as expressing *when* some activity took place, many languages also express other temporal features of the activity – for example, its duration, whether the action is complete, and whether it is a repetitive action. These are all types of 'aspect'.

English makes a distinction between 'perfect' and 'progressive' aspect, for example. A sentence such as *'She has read the book'* has perfect aspect, which indicates that an activity is completed. *'She was reading the book'*, on the other hand, has progressive aspect, indicating that the activity takes place over a period of time, with no indication of whether it is completed or not. Some languages have both tense and aspect, others have only one or other of these and some languages (such as Chinese) have neither.

In many languages it can be difficult to draw a clear distinction between tense and aspect and because of this some linguists prefer to use a single notion of tense–aspect.

see also...

Mood and modality; Tense; Verb

Assimilation

'**A**ssimilation' is the influence that one sound exerts on an adjacent sound, with the result that the two sounds become more similar. For example, the negative prefix -*un* is pronounced [un] in the word *untruthful*, [ung] in *uncomfortable* and [um] in *unbelievable*. In each case, the /n/ assimilates to the following sound, taking on the same place of articulation. Thus, the initial [b] sound of *believable* is pronounced with both lips brought together (it is 'bilabial'), and the /n/ of the prefix therefore changes to an [m], which is also bilabial. Similarly, the initial [k] sound of *comfortable* is pronounced with the back of the tongue touching the roof of the mouth (it is 'velar'), and so the /n/ of the prefix changes to [ng], which is also velar. In the word *untruthful*, both [n] and [t] are pronounced at the same place, so no change occurs.

As well as occurring within words, assimilation can also occur between words. For example, in normal speech the phrase *ten maps* would be pronounced [tem maps]. In this case the assimilation is total, and the two sounds have become identical. (In the previous example, the assimilation was only partial.) Notice that in these examples it is always the first sound that changes to become more like the following sound. This is known as 'anticipatory assimilation'. It is also possible (although less common) for a sound to change under the influence of the preceding sound.

There are various reasons for sound changes such as assimilation. One reason is to do with the physical process of speaking. While they are producing one sound, the muscles controlling the movement of the speech organs have already received instructions from the brain to produce the next sound. Minimisation of effort leads to adjacent sounds being pronounced more alike.

---

see also...

Distinctive feature; Phoneme; Phonology; Place of articulation

Auxiliary

Many languages alter the form of verbs (often adding particular endings) to indicate various kinds of grammatical information, such as tense and mood. In some languages, however, it is necessary to use an additional verb to convey this information. For example, English verbs have no way of indicating mood and so we need to use an additional verb such as *should*, *may* or *must* to express mood (as in the sentences *'I should go'* or *'You must sleep'*). These additional verbs are known as 'auxiliaries'.

Auxiliaries have different grammatical properties from main verbs. For example, in English they have a special negative form (e.g. *couldn't*, *won't*, *hasn't*), whereas main verbs do not (so we cannot say **eatn't*). Also, we can form questions by 'inverting' the subject and the auxiliary (*he does* becomes *does he?* and *he will* becomes *will he?*), but we cannot do this with main verbs (*he eats* cannot become **eats he?*).

In English, there are four types of auxiliary: 'primary auxiliaries' (such as *be* and *have*) which are also able to act as main verbs; 'modal auxiliaries' (such as *can, will, should, might*) which express mood (as well as other distinctions such as tense and aspect); 'semi-modals' (such as *dare* and *need*) which show some, but not all, of the properties of auxiliaries; and the 'dummy' auxiliary *do*, which is used to form questions, negatives and so on when there is no other auxiliary in the sentence (as in *'She **does**n't like fish'* or *'**Do** you like fish?'*).

> ### see also...
>
> *Grammatical category; Mood and modality; Verb*

Bilingualism

Anyone who can speak two languages can be said to be 'bilingual' (people who speak three or more languages are known as 'multilingual'). The term is often reserved, however, for people who speak two native languages, usually because they have grown up in a family or community in which more than one language is routinely spoken. While it is regarded as somewhat unusual in English-speaking countries, over two-thirds of the world's population are thought to be bilingual or multilingual.

It is remarkable that young children have no difficulty in acquiring two or more languages at the same time. Imagine trying to learn a language from a teacher who spoke in a mixture of Japanese and Chinese, but did not explain when she was speaking which language or even how many different languages she was speaking in! This task seems almost impossible, but is achieved by infants with apparent ease. How do they manage this? Psycholinguists believe that a number of factors may help the child. Often, the different languages are spoken in different situations. For example, one parent may tend to use one particular language or the child may hear one language at school and another at home. This cannot be the whole story, however, and in some cases the child must use characteristics of the languages themselves to help distinguish one language from another.

Bilingualism is also investigated by sociolinguists studying what happens when speakers of different languages come into contact. Bilingualism is one of the most obvious results of language contact and is clearly a highly effective solution to the problems raised by such contact.

see also...

Acquisition of language; Language contact; Psycholinguistics; Sociolinguistics

Bloomfield, Leonard

Leonard Bloomfield (1887–1949) was Professor of Linguistics at Chicago and Yale universities and was the most prominent American linguist of his generation. His 1933 book *Language* was the standard introduction to linguistics for many years. He established the school of thought known as 'American structuralism', which dominated linguistics until the advent of Chomsky's transformational–generative grammar in the 1950s.

Bloomfield was greatly influenced by behaviourism, the school of psychology that rejected mental notions and tried to refer only to observable behaviour in its explanations. This led Bloomfield to reject the traditional view that the structure of language reflects the structure of thought. He argued that all linguistic structure could be determined by the careful analysis of spoken language. This extremely rigorous approach led to major advances in the study of the sound systems ('phonology') and the grammatical structure ('morphology' and 'syntax') of language.

In restricting linguistics to the study of observable behaviour, however, Bloomfield was unable to give any satisfactory account of the meaning of language ('semantics'). This was to lead ultimately to the collapse of structuralism. The end came in 1957, when Chomsky published a review of the book *Verbal Behavior* by leading behaviourist B. F. Skinner. The review was widely seen as devastating for behaviourism and persuaded most linguists that structuralism should be rejected.

see also...

Chomsky; Transformational–generative grammar

Case

The case of a word or phrase indicates its relationship to other words in the sentence. Consider the sentence *'He hit John in the ribs with his elbow'*. In this sentence *he* is the 'subject', *John* is the 'object', *his* is a 'possessive', *in the ribs* is a 'locative' and *with his elbow* is an 'instrumental'. Languages have different ways of marking such case relationships.

Sometimes languages use 'morphological case', where changes in the form of the word (its 'morphology') indicate different cases. English uses this method to indicate the case of pronouns (for example, the third-person pronoun in English has three forms: *he* when used as a subject, *his* when used as a possessive, and *him* elsewhere). Nouns in Latin, German and other languages (but not English) also have morphological case; in Latin there are different endings for nominative (which marks subjects), accusative (which marks direct objects), genitive (which marks possessives), dative (which marks indirect objects) and ablative (which marks instrumentals and locatives). Finnish has as many as 16 different morphological cases.

Languages can also use prepositions to mark case. In the English example above, *with* marks an instrumental and *in* marks a locative. Often, however, languages do not mark these case relationships overtly at all. In such situations, other information such as word order must be used to identify syntactic relationships. In the English sentence *'The dog chased the cat'*, for example, subject and object are indicated not by prepositions or morphological markings but by word order (hence *'The cat chased the dog'* means something very different). Languages with a rich system of morphological cases do not need to rely on word order to indicate case and hence their word order can be relatively free.

see also...

Morphology; Noun; Object; Preposition; Sentence; Subject; Syntax; Word order

Chomsky, Noam

Avram Noam Chomsky (b. 1928) is Institute Professor at the Department of Linguistics and Philosophy, Massachusetts Institute of Technology. He is the most influential modern linguist and revolutionised the field with the publication in 1957 of his monograph *Syntactic Structures*, which introduced his theory of transformational–generative grammar. He went on to publish a series of books and articles detailing and advancing the theory, including *Aspects of the Theory of Syntax* (1965), *Reflections on Language* (1976), *Knowledge of Language* (1986) and *The Minimalist Program* (1995).

In arguing the view that linguistics should be seen as a branch of cognitive psychology, Chomsky also came to be extremely influential in disciplines such as philosophy and psychology. He argued strenuously against the behaviourist view of language learning, according to which we learn a language by associating words with stimuli. Chomsky pointed out that this could not explain how, after hearing relatively few utterances, children gain the creative ability to understand and produce infinitely many grammatical sentences. Chomsky also stresses the similarities shared by all human languages (compared with the diverse range of imaginable languages), which he believes arise from an innate 'universal grammar' that all humans are born with. This explains not only why all human languages are so similar, but also how children are able to acquire language so quickly and easily.

Chomsky has also been an influential political commentator and he is probably as widely known for his politics as for his linguistics.

see also...

*Acquisition of language;
Transformational–generative
grammar; Universal grammar*

Clause

Some sentences seem to contain other sentences within them. For example, in the sentence *'I wonder whether I should go to work tomorrow'*, the words *I should go to work tomorrow* seem to have the same structure as a sentence: there is a subject, a verb and an object (and, in this case at least, they could form an independent sentence on their own). Such structures are known as clauses.

Sentences consist of one or more clauses. A 'simple sentence' such as *'Dogs chase cats'* contains a single clause (the sentence itself). So-called 'compound sentences' contain two or more clauses joined by a connecting word such as *and* or *but* (e.g. *'[Dogs chase cats] and [cats chase mice]'*). 'Complex sentences' are those where the sentence consists of a clause within a clause (e.g. *'[The claim [that Elvis is alive] is false]'* or *'[John hates [getting up early]]'*); in this case, the whole sentence is known as the 'main clause', and the clause within it is known as a 'subordinate clause'.

There are several kinds of subordinate clause. For example, a clause that modifies a noun is known as a

'relative clause' (e.g. *'[The dog [that lives next door] bites the postman]'*). A subordinate clause that has the form of a question is known as a 'wh-clause' (e.g. *'[I wonder [why John chose that car?]]'*).

see also...

Phrase; Sentence

Communication

As you read these words, a remarkable thing is happening. Ink marks on paper are allowing me to communicate my thoughts to you, although we are separated by both time and space. This is being achieved through the medium of language, and language is clearly a very useful tool for communication. But communication can take many forms, not all of them involving language. For example, I can communicate danger to someone by shouting *'Watch out!'*, but I can also wave my hands in the air or run away screaming from the source of the danger. It is important to note, however, that language has other uses besides communication – it also has an important role in thought, for example. So while the study of language is clearly related to the study of communication, they are not one and the same thing.

Suppose that I want you to do something (say, close the window). I might communicate this to you by uttering a sentence such as *'It's a bit cold in here'*, which will hopefully result in you closing the window. But note that what I have actually said does not mean 'close the window' (in a different context, it might merely be a comment about the temperature). What has happened is that you have inferred from my statement, together with other information (such as the fact that the window is open) that I would like the window closed. I might have communicated this just as effectively by shivering in an obvious way and blowing on my fingers, however. Communication involves inferring what people mean, but this process may or may not involve language.

see also...

Pragmatics

20

Competence and performance

Imagine a physicist giving an analysis of some physical system — say a ball rolling down a slope. In order to analyse and describe the behaviour of the ball, the physicist would typically make certain idealisations, ignoring the effects of wind resistance, friction and so on. Similarly, Chomsky has argued that when linguists analyse our mental grammar they should also make idealisations: they should ignore errors such as slips of the tongue, false starts (when we change our minds about what we want to say part way through a sentence), failing to hear what is said and the effects of limited memory.

Chomsky's position is that these errors are not for linguists to analyse, since they are largely caused by systems having nothing to do with language: muscle control, memory, and so on. Linguistics should give an account of our abstract competence, or knowledge, rather than our performance. In the same way that someone can know how to ride a bicycle, even when they have a broken leg and cannot actually ride one, a person knows which sentences are grammatical, even though they may make certain errors when they produce these sentences.

Chomsky's arguments have been very influential and are now widely accepted. His distinction between competence and performance is somewhat similar to Saussure's distinction between 'langue' and 'parole', although the latter were not defined in mental terms.

see also...

Chomsky; Saussure; Transformational–generative grammar

Complement

Languages create larger constituents by combining smaller ones – they combine words to form phrases and they combine phrases to form clauses and sentences. Words, phrases and clauses are not the only constituents, however. Consider the following expressions: *student of linguistics* and *student with red shoes*. In each case we have a noun (*student*) that has combined with a preposition phrase (*of linguistics* or *with red shoes*) to form a larger constituent.

There are important differences, however, between the expressions *student of linguistics* and *student with red shoes*. A student must be a student *of* something, so there is a sense in which *of linguistics* completes the meaning of *student*. For this reason, phrases such as *of linguistics* are known as 'complements'. A student, however, does not need to have red shoes, so there is no sense in which *with red shoes* completes the meaning of *student*. Phrases such as *with red shoes* are known as 'adjuncts'.

There are several grammatical differences between complements and adjuncts. A head (such as a noun, verb, preposition and so on) combines first with its complements, if it has any, to form a constituent. Only then can this constituent combine with adjuncts. For example, we can combine a head such as *student* with a complement such as *of linguistics* to form the constituent *student of linguistics*. Only then can we add the adjunct *with red shoes*, to form *student of linguistics with red shoes*. If we try to combine the head with the adjunct first, and then with the complement, the result is ungrammatical: **student with red shoes of linguistics*.

see also...

Adjunct; Constituent; Head; Phrase

Consonant

peech sounds are divided into two categories: 'consonants' and 'vowels'. Consonants are defined as sounds made by a narrowing or closure of the vocal tract, resulting in the airflow being either completely blocked or restricted so much that friction sound is produced. For example, try saying the sound [p]. You will feel your lips close to block the air flow, then open suddenly to release the air. Now say the sound [f]. In this case, the airflow is not completely blocked – some air flows between your teeth and your lip, making a friction sound.

As well as the above phonetic description, it is also possible to define consonants according to how they function in sound systems (i.e. according to their phonological properties). Normally, these two ways of defining consonants coincide, but there is one problematic class of sounds, known as 'approximants' (e.g. sounds such as [w], [r] and [l]). These sounds are phonetically vowels, because they are produced with no constriction of the airflow. They behave as if they were consonants, however: we have pairs of words such as *pat* and *rat*, or *wet* and *net*, where

it is clear that the approximant is in a consonant position. These sounds are therefore classified as a kind of consonant, although they are often known as 'semi-vowels' or 'semi-consonants'.

Consonants are classified according to their place and manner of articulation, as well as whether they are 'voiced' (produced with vibrating vocal cords, like [b]), or 'voiceless' (like [p]). It is sometimes also necessary to specify their duration, and certain properties of the air stream.

see also...

Manner of articulation; Phonology; Place of articulation; Vowel

Constituent

Sentences do not consist of merely sequences of words. Words are first combined to form phrases and phrases are then combined to form clauses and sentences. This process is governed by the grammar of the language. For linguists who wish to discover what the grammatical rules of a particular language are, it is necessary to have methods for determining the structure of sentences. Clauses, phrases and other parts of sentence structure are known as 'constituents'.

Consider a sentence such as *'Piglet dislikes very large animals'*. This is made up of two constituents: *Piglet* (the 'subject') and *dislikes very large animals* (the 'verb phrase' or 'predicate'). The first constituent cannot be broken down any further, but the second constituent can be split into further constituents (the verb *dislikes* and the noun phrase *very large animals*). This process can be continued until we are left with just individual words. The resulting structure can be shown using a 'tree diagram'.

Linguists have various ways of determining whether or not a certain sequence of words is a constituent. For example, if the words can be moved to a different place in the sentence, this is evidence that they form a constituent. Thus, a sentence like *'Piglet dislikes animals which are **very large**'* shows that *very large* is a constituent. Similarly, if the words can be replaced by a single word, this is further evidence that they form a constituent. According to this test, *very large animals* is also a constituent, since it can be replaced by *what* in the sentence *'Piglet dislikes **what?**'*.

see also...

Syntax; Tree diagram

Creoles and pidgins

When speakers of two different languages meet, they often develop a crude method of communication by stringing together words from both languages in simple structures. In this way, a simplified language known as a 'pidgin' develops and this can become the language of interaction of the two communities. Pidgins develop most commonly in situations of colonisation or trade. They are not spoken by anyone as a native language, have a very simple structure and are typically used for a limited range of functions (such as trade).

Sometimes a pidgin can increase in complexity over time, as it becomes more generally used. An interesting thing happens, however, when children grow up in a community where a pidgin is spoken. They begin to acquire it as a native language and as they do so they 'invent' a complex structure to fill in the gaps in the pidgin. In this way, the pidgin is transformed into a language as complex as any other, by a single generation of children. The resulting language is known as a 'creole'. Most of the present-day languages around the world known as pidgins are in fact creoles.

But how do children 'invent' complex structures when they only hear simple strings of words? The answer seems to be that children are born with information about what a language should look like (which is why they are able to acquire their native language with such apparent ease). This information, when combined with the pidgin language they hear, enables them to construct a fully functional language. Of course, they do this subconsciously, much in the same way as they develop other basic skills such as walking.

see also...

Acquisition of language;
Bilingualism; Language contact

Deep and surface structure

Deep structure (or 'd-structure') is an important aspect of the theory of transformational–generative grammar introduced by Chomsky in the 1950s. Grammatical sentences must conform to rules laid down by the grammar. (These are rules represented in the mind of every speaker of the language and have nothing to do with the prescriptive 'rules' laid down by some traditional grammarians, such as 'Never end a sentence with a preposition'.) For example, a transitive verb requires both a subject and a direct object. But certain sentences seem to violate this rule: for example, the verb *make* is transitive (we cannot say **I made*), but we find sentences such as *'Mistakes were made'*, which are perfectly grammatical, but which appear to lack an object.

To account for such sentences, Chomsky proposed that there is more than one level at which grammatical rules can apply. The first level he called 'deep structure'. At this level, verbs must have the correct subject and objects, for example (so the deep structure for the sentence above might be something like *'Someone made mistakes'*). Since the rules for subjects and objects are satisfied by deep structure, other rules called 'transformations' can then apply to insert, delete and move parts of the sentence. In the present case, the subject *someone* is deleted, the object *mistakes* is moved to subject position, and *were* is inserted. The resulting structure is known as the 'surface structure' and is what we actually hear (or speak). Deep structure allows linguists to make generalisations which they would not otherwise be able to make. Not all linguists agree that deep structure is needed, however.

see also...

Chomsky; Transformational–generative grammar

Deixis (indexical)

Imagine you are walking along the beach one day and you find a bottle, in which there is a message: *'Come and help me, I've been marooned on this island for six months now!'* Although this message is perfectly understandable, it is unlikely to help the unlucky castaway. You cannot tell who has written the message, which island they are marooned on or even how long they have been there (since you do not know how long the message has been at sea; it may have been written years ago).

What has gone wrong is this: the message contains several words known as 'deictics' (also called 'indexicals'), which refer directly to aspects of the situation in which an utterance takes place. Examples of deictics are pronouns (for example, *me* and *I* in the message, which refer to the person who wrote the message), some determiners (for example *this* in the message, which refers to some object in the location where the message was written) and some adverbs (for example *now* in the message, which refers to the time the message was written).

Other forms of deixis are less obvious. For example, the verb *come* in the message above also carries deictic information – it means something like 'move to the location where the message was written'. The tense of verbs is also deictic, since it refers to when the action described by the verb took place, relative to the time of the utterance.

As well as referring to the time and location of a situation, deictics can also encode social relations (such as when we use *my lord* to address a judge) or refer to elements in a text (for example *the former* or *the undersigned*).

see also...

Adverb; Determiner; Pronoun and proform; Tense; Utterance; Verb

Determiner

Words such as *the, this, my* and *any*, which most commonly occur with nouns to express properties such as quantity, are members of the class of determiners. The most common determiners are the articles (*a/an/the* in English), and other determiners are classified on the basis that they occur in the same position as the articles (e.g. we can have *a book, this book, my book* or *any book*). These other determiners cannot occur at the same time as an article in English (so we cannot have **the my book*). Possessives such as *my* are traditionally called 'possessive pronouns'; in fact they are not pronouns, but determiners.

As well as occurring before nouns, many determiners can also be used on their own, without any following noun. For example, as well as *'I don't like this book'* we can also have *'I don't like this'*. It is also possible to have sequences of two determiners, such as *'all these books'*, but only a few determiners have the ability to occur before another determiner in this way.

Many determiners express quantity (e.g. *some, all, several*) and these are sometimes known as 'quantifiers'. Quantifiers have a particularly important role to play in logic. Some linguists prefer to view quantifiers as a separate word class, but there are no particularly strong reasons for doing so.

see also...

Logic and linguistics; Part of speech

Dialect

It may seem fairly obvious what a dialect is – a regional variation of a language. On this view, human speech can be divided into distinct languages and languages in turn can be divided into dialects. This sort of view is widespread, but in fact it is impossible to draw a clear distinction between languages and dialects in this way. For example, Dutch and German are considered separate languages – no one would ever speak of Dutch as being a 'dialect of German' or vice versa. But actually these languages are mutually intelligible to a large degree. Mandarin, Cantonese and Hakka, in contrast, are generally regarded as dialects of Chinese, although they are mutually unintelligible. As one well-known linguist put it: a language is a dialect with an army and a navy.

The point is that *everyone* speaks a very slightly different language from everyone else. Where groups of people share something in common then their language often has certain similarities as well. When people who share a geographical location speak similarly, we term it a 'dialect'; if they share a social grouping, we speak of a 'register'. From a linguistic point of view, however, the terms 'language' and 'dialect' are largely meaningless. At what point do differences in language between groups of speakers become great enough that we should recognise their speech as a separate dialect or a separate language? The decision has to be made largely on social or political grounds (for example, it might be a question of group identity), but it is not possible to make such a decision on purely linguistic grounds.

see also...

Language; Register

Discourse

When we use language, we combine words to form phrases and we combine phrases to form clauses and sentences. Sentences may also be combined to form larger stretches of language known as 'discourse' (for example, conversations, stories, jokes, letters and so on). Linguists are interested in the ways in which discourse is structured and used.

There are three particular aspects of discourse investigated by linguists. First, discourse may be seen as a verbal exchange made in a social and cultural context. Sociolinguists investigate how people negotiate turn-taking, the beginning and end of a conversation and shifts in topic within the conversation. Second, the linguistic content of the discourse may be analysed. This is known as 'discourse analysis', and tries to formulate rules governing how sentences may be combined (for example, the ways in which expressions such as *she, it, therefore,* or *the aforementioned* may be used to create links between different parts of the discourse). Third, the investigation of discourse is important in pragmatics. Here, the focus is on uncovering principles of human communication. Of particular interest is how discourse enables information to be communicated in particular contexts. For example, if someone asks *'Would you like tea or coffee?'*, the reply *'Coffee keeps me awake'* might be interpreted as a request for tea in certain contexts (e.g. late at night before going to bed), but a request for coffee in others (e.g. late at night while studying for an exam).

> ## see also...
> *Pragmatics; Sociolinguistics*

Distinctive feature

Just as physicists used to think that atoms were the smallest unit of matter, linguists used to think that individual sounds ('phonemes') such as /n/, /l/ and /a/ were the smallest units of language. One problem with this view, however, was that it did not allow any systematic way of classifying sounds in terms of their similarity. It was Jakobson who first proposed that phonemes could be split into smaller units. These units, called 'distinctive features', are now defined in articulatory terms (i.e. in terms of activities of the speech organs). For example, the phoneme /n/ is composed of the features [+nasal] (air passes through the nose), [−continuant] (air is blocked from passing through the mouth) and [+coronal] (tongue tip is elevated). All features are binary (that is, they can only be marked as present or absent, using a plus sign or a minus sign).

Distinctive feature theory is not just a way of describing sounds, it is a hypothesis about how speech sounds are represented in the mind. It is thought that about 20 features are needed for the sounds of all the world's languages and together these features define what is a possible speech sound. Other sounds that we can make quite easily, such as coughs and burps, are not possible speech sounds because they are not made up of distinctive features. Research into sign languages indicates that these too can be analysed in terms of distinctive features (although the individual features are different, since they refer to activities of the hands and upper body, rather than the speech organs).

see also...

Jakobson; Phoneme; Phonology; Sign language

Focus

Important new information in an utterance can be identified by using stress. The element of the utterance which receives stress in such cases is said to be the 'focus' of the utterance. For example, the sentence *'John walked to the park'* can be uttered with the focus on different elements: *'JOHN walked to the park (not Bill)'*, *'John WALKed to the park (he didn't drive)'*, or *'John walked to the PARK (not the beach)'*. As well as identifying new information, focus is also often seen as indicating that there are alternatives to the item in focus (such as the information in brackets in the above sentences).

Focus can often be ambiguous. For example, when a notorious bank robber was asked by a journalist *'Why do you rob banks?'*, he replied *'Because that's where the money is'*. Clearly the journalist had been asking *'Why do you ROB BANKS (rather than selling insurance, say)?'*, but the bank robber had replied as if the journalist had asked *'Why do you rob BANKS (rather than corner shops, say)'*. These two utterances sound the same, because even when *rob banks* is focused, only the word *banks* is actually stressed.

Although focus is typically marked with stress in spoken language, some languages mark focus syntactically. For example, in American Sign Language, focus is marked with a brow raise and in the South American language Quechua, it is marked with a specific particle. It is important not to confuse focus with the somewhat similar notion of the 'topic' of a sentence (which is not stressed).

see also...

Stress; Topic

Frege, Gottlob

ottlob Frege (1848–1925) was Professor of Mathematics at the University of Jena. He was the father of modern mathematical logic and philosophy of language, and his work has had enormous influence in semantics.

Two semantic puzzles particularly intrigued Frege and both still constitute major problems for theories of meaning. The first puzzle related to identity statements such as *Mohammad Ali is Cassius Clay*. A popular idea is that the meaning of an expression is what it refers to. But *Mohammad Ali* and *Cassius Clay* refer to the same person, so the sentence should have the same meaning as the totally uninformative sentence *Mohammad Ali is Mohammad Ali*. Clearly this is not the case, however. Frege's conclusion was that there must be more to the meaning of an expression than its reference. He called this extra something the 'sense' of an expression.

Frege's second puzzle involved sentences such as *John believes that Mohammad Ali is Mohammad Ali*. This sentence is presumably true, even if John knows nothing about boxing. Standard logic tells us that if an expression in a sentence is substituted with another expression referring to the same thing, then the truth of the sentence does not change. But if we do this in the above sentence we end up with *John believes that Mohammad Ali is Cassius Clay*, which may well be false (if John is not a boxing fan, say). Frege's conclusion was that standard logic could not be applied in certain contexts – something which causes great difficulties for theories of meaning.

see also...

Logic and linguistics; Semantics

Gender

In some languages, nouns are divided into different classes known as 'genders'. In German, for example, nouns may be 'masculine', 'feminine' or 'neuter'. These different genders require different forms of adjectives and determiners – so we have *der Löffel* 'the spoon', *die Feder* 'the pen' and *das Messer* 'the knife'. The word for 'the' is different in each case: *der* is used with masculine nouns, *die* with feminine nouns, and *das* with neuter nouns.

The term 'gender' is somewhat misleading, since there need not be any correlation between the grammatical gender of a noun and the biological sex of the object it refers to (and, in any case, many objects such as spoons and pens have no biological sex). In many European languages there *is* some correlation between gender and sex, in the sense that nouns for things that are clearly male (e.g. 'boy', 'son') have one gender, while nouns for things that are clearly female (e.g. 'woman', 'aunt') have another. But in many languages there is no correlation at all. For example, some Bantu languages have as many as 16 genders, with nouns being assigned to one of these classes on the basis of animacy, shape, size and so on.

So, while in some languages we can predict the gender of a noun on the basis of the sex of the object it refers to, or on the basis of other criteria such as size or shape of the object, this is not always reliable. It is sometimes also possible to predict gender from the form of the noun itself (e.g. in some Australian languages gender depends on the number of syllables a noun has). In most cases, however, gender is completely unpredictable and must simply be learned.

see also...

Grammatical category; Noun

Grammar

The word *glamour* comes from the word *grammar*. But for most people grammar is anything but glamorous, conjuring up memories of dull schoolbooks warning about the dire consequences of splitting infinitives. Linguists use the term in a different way. For them, the grammar of a language is not a collection of rules laid down by teachers about how to speak properly, but rather the information we have in our minds that gives us the ability to speak a language.

While the word 'grammar' is sometimes used just to include syntax and morphology, it is more commonly used in linguistics to refer to the entire system of knowledge that a person must possess about their language. This includes the lexicon (a list of words), phonology (information about pronunciation), morphology (information about word structure), syntax (information about phrase and sentence structure), and semantics (information about meaning). Pragmatic information (how we use language in context) is not usually taken to be part of the grammar. Many aspects of grammar are thought to be hardwired into the brains of all humans and hence to be universal.

There are several competing theories of grammar, including 'transformational–generative grammar', 'lexical–functional grammar' and several versions of 'phrase-structure grammar'. These are not grammars of particular languages, but theories about what form our mental grammar takes.

see also...

Transformational–generative grammar; Universal grammar

Grammatical category

In English, nouns carry information about whether they are singular or plural (although there are a few exceptions such as *sheep*). Whenever we want to talk about dogs, for example, we must use the word *dog* or the word *dogs*. Similarly, whenever we use a verb in English, it must be in the past tense (e.g. *went*) or the present tense (*go*). Grammatical notions such as plurality ('number') or tense, which are expressed by modifying the form of a word, are known as 'grammatical categories'.

Grammatical categories usually apply to a particular word class. For example, tense, aspect and mood apply to verbs, whereas person, number, case and gender apply to nouns. Not all grammatical categories occur in all languages. For example, English nouns indicate only the category of number, whereas in many other languages nouns also have different forms for different cases, different genders and so on.

Some grammatical categories are taken to be universal. For example, many linguists believe that the category of case is universal, even though some languages do not actually mark case on the noun. Other categories are probably not universal. For example, some languages must mark whether or not an object referred to is visible to the speaker.

Often, a grammatical category which must be marked on a particular word class in one language may be optionally marked in other ways by another language. For example, some languages must indicate 'aspect' – e.g., whether a particular activity happens repeatedly or not – by using a particular verb form. This is not obligatory in English, but we can express this using an adverb if we want: *'John is **always** getting sick'*.

see also...

Aspect; Case; Grammar; Part of Speech

Grice, H. Paul

The work of H. Paul Grice (1913–1988) was an English philosopher whose work has been very influential in linguistics, particularly in pragmatics. He introduced a fundamental distinction between 'speaker meaning' and 'linguistic meaning'. Consider the sentence *'I'm feeling a bit tired'*. The linguistic meaning of the sentence is just that the speaker is feeling a bit tired, but the speaker meaning (what the speaker intended to communicate) might be very different, for example *'I don't want to see a movie'*. This distinction is the basis for the separation of semantics from pragmatics.

Grice saw communication as a cooperative enterprise involving speaker and hearer. He proposed that communication was governed by the following 'cooperative principle': Make your conversational contribution such as is required, at the stage at which it occurs, by the accepted purpose or direction of the talk exchange in which you are engaged. He developed this principle into a theory of communication based on a number of maxims, which he classified into four categories: 'maxims of quantity' (*be informative, but not more so than is required*); 'maxims of quality' (*say only what you believe to be true*); 'maxims of relevance' (*be relevant*); and 'maxims of manner' (*be perspicuous*). Grice's idea was that the hearer of an utterance could use these maxims to eliminate all meanings other than the speaker's intended meaning.

see also...

Communication; Pragmatics; Semantics

Head

In order to form sentences, words are combined into larger structures called phrases, according to principles laid down in the grammar of the language. Every phrase contains an element (usually a word) around which the rest of the phrase is constructed. This element is known as the 'head' of the phrase and it determines many of the grammatical properties of the phrase. For example, in the phrase *healthy people* the noun *people* is the head, so this phrase would be a noun phrase. In the phrase *eat vegetables*, the most important element is the verb *eat*, so this is the head and this phrase is a verb phrase. All parts of speech can act as the head of a phrase (so we also find preposition phrases such as *over the top*, and adjective phrases such as *extremely happy*, for example). Conversely, all phrases must have a head.

The head of a phrase can be identified in various ways. One way is that the head is obligatory. Thus, in the adjective phrase *extremely happy* the adjective *happy* cannot be omitted, whereas the adverb *extremely* can be (e.g. in the sentence 'The boy is extremely happy' we could omit *extremely* to form 'The boy is happy', but we could not omit *happy* to form *'The boy is extremely'*). The head of a phrase also determines what other words can appear in the phrase. For example, the verb *sell* requires an object, so we have the verb phrase *sold a book*, but not the verb phrase **sold* (we can see this from the fact that the sentence 'I sold a book' is grammatical, whereas **I sold* is not). The verb *sleep*, on the other hand, does not require an object, so we can have the verb phrase *slept* (e.g. in a sentence such as 'I slept').

see also...
Adjunct; Complement; Phrase

Historical linguistics

Around 100 years before Darwin formulated his theory of evolution, linguists noticed that Greek, Latin and Sanskrit have a great many features in common and proposed that each had evolved gradually, through a series of small changes, from a single parent language. This work in the 1780s marked the beginning of historical linguistics (traditionally known as 'comparative philology'), the field that investigates how languages change over time.

Greek, Latin and Sanskrit, along with many other languages of Europe and South Asia, are members of the 'Indo-European' language family. They are all descended from a single language known as 'Proto-Indo-European'. Linguists are able to identify language families by looking for common features among languages. For example, Greek, Latin and Sanskrit have many similar words (e.g. *brother* is *phrater*, *frater* and *bhrater* in these languages; for *is* we find *esti*, *est* and *asti*). There are so many similarities between the various Indo-European languages that linguists have been able to reconstruct a hypothetical dictionary and grammar for Proto-Indo-European, even though this language was never recorded. This is possible because language change is not erratic – for example, the sound /p/ in Proto-Indo–European consistently became /f/ in Germanic, but did not change in other language groups (which is why we find *pater* in Latin, *piter* in Sanskrit, but *father* in English). Historical linguists are interested in discovering the principles behind such language change and the reasons why some types of change are more likely than others.

Recent evidence suggests that language change does not happen at a uniform rate, but that there are periods of abrupt change followed by longer periods of relative stability.

see also...

Language family; Typology

Homonymy and polysemy

Words often have more than one meaning. For example, the English word *bank* may refer to the ground beside a river or to a financial institution, and *mouth* may refer to a part of the body, a part of a river or the entrance to a cave.

It seems that there are differences, however, between the case of *bank* and the case of *mouth*. The two meanings of *bank* seem to be unrelated and it is just an accident that the two words happen to have the same form (etymology supports this idea, since the two meanings have different historical origins). Cases such as this, where the similarity in the pronunciation (or spelling) of a word is accidental are known as 'homonymy'.

In the case of *mouth*, however, the relation between the different meanings is fairly clear. The mouth is an entrance into the body and the metaphorical similarity between this notion and the notion of the mouth of a cave or the mouth of a river is fairly obvious. Cases such as this, where a word has a number of related meanings, are known as 'polysemy'.

While in principle the difference between homonymy and polysemy is clear, in practice it can be very difficult to draw the distinction. The main issue for linguists is whether in such cases there is a single item in a person's mental lexicon that expresses different shades of meaning in different contexts or whether the separate meanings are listed as separate lexical items.

see also...

Ambiguity; Lexicon

Interjection

Words such as *Yuk!*, *Hell!*, *hmm* and *tut-tut* are known as 'interjections'. Some of these words can only be used as interjections (e.g. *Yuk!*), while others can have other uses (e.g. *hell* is also a noun). Interjections are spontaneous, often involuntary expressions of emotion and do not seem to be a part of language proper. They are used in isolation, do not combine with other words and may violate normal rules governing which sound combinations can occur in words (e.g. *hmm*).

In many ways interjections are more like screams, smiles or nods than words. For example, if I hit my thumb with a hammer, I am more likely to cry out or say *'Hell!'* (or worse) than use a linguistic expression such as *'I have hit my thumb and it hurts'*.

Psycholinguistic evidence supports the idea that interjections are not fully linguistic. Some patients with severe brain damage completely lose the ability to use language, but may continue to use interjections. Also, some people with Tourette's Syndrome suffer from 'coprolalia', the uncontrollable shouting of interjections (particularly obscenities).

Neurological studies have indicated that these uses of interjections are not controlled by the language areas of the brain, but by older structures that control things such as sobbing and laughing (and the vocal calls of primates).

> ## *see also...*
> *Morphology; Part of speech*

International Phonetic Alphabet

In English, we write down words using the letters *a* to *z*. This is not very useful for linguists who want to record sounds, however. First, alphabets are not usually systematic (the letter 'c' in English can represent the sounds [k] and [s], for example). Second, alphabets are not very accurate (so the letter 'p' sounds different in *pin* and *spin*). Third, some languages do not have a written form and, even when they do, this may not represent the sound of the words (as in the case of Chinese characters). Linguists therefore need an accurate and systematic way of transcribing speech sounds that can be used for all languages. By far the most commonly used system is the International Phonetic Alphabet (IPA).

The IPA tries to use a separate symbol for each distinctive sound and this same symbol should be used for that sound in any language that uses it. This means that there are a large number of separate symbols (over 100), but a much smaller number is needed for each individual language.

The IPA is based on the Roman alphabet, supplemented with other symbols and 'diacritics' (accents and other marks written above or below letters). It was invented in 1888, but has been frequently revised and expanded since then. It is now widely used outside linguistics, for example in dictionaries and languages texts. As well as accurately representing particular sounds, IPA can also be used to represent phonemes. In order to distinguish between the two, phonemes are written between slashes (e.g. /t/), whereas accurate representations of sounds are written in square brackets (e.g. [tʰ]).

see also...

Phoneme; Phonetics

Intonation

In writing, we use punctuation to indicate whether something is a statement, a question or an exclamation. This is necessary because our writing system is not able to capture all aspects of our speech – it records individual sounds, but not, for example, the characteristic rise and fall of our voice associated with statements, questions and so on. These variations of pitch during speech are known as 'intonation'.

Intonation can be used to convey various kinds of information. Its most important role has already been mentioned: it is used to signal grammatical structure, rather like punctuation (although it involves far more contrasts). For example, a sentence such as *'You're leaving now'* can be uttered as an order with one intonation pattern (falling pitch) or as a question with another intonation pattern (rising pitch). The structure of a sentence is also indicated by pauses between phrases or clauses (rather like the way we use commas in writing). Intonation is also used to indicate attitudes of the speaker, such as irony, disbelief or anger.

Particular patterns of intonation do not appear to be universal. For example, not all languages indicate questions with a rising pitch at the end. Also, not all languages use variations of pitch to convey just information about utterances (such as whether they are questions or statements). Some languages, known as tone languages, use variations of pitch to change the meanings of individual words and these languages usually make only limited use of intonation.

---

see also...

Phonetics; Phonology; Stress; Tone and tone language

Irony

anguage can be used to communicate something other than what it literally means, as when a question (*'Can you pass the salt?'*) is used to communicate a request ('Please pass the salt'). It seems that language can even be used to communicate the opposite of what it literally means, as in ironical utterances such as *'You're so clever'* (although not all ironical utterances communicate the exact opposite of what they literally mean).

But how is this possible? Clearly, there is not a general rule of interpretation which says 'sentences may be used to communicate the opposite of what they literally mean'. If this were the case, we could say *no* to mean *yes* and expect to be understood and we could in general say the opposite of what we meant. So how can we understand ironical utterances?

Consider an example. Suppose Peter is fixing Sarah's computer and generally bragging about how clever he is, when his screwdriver slips, damaging the circuit board. Sarah says: *'You're so clever'*. What Sarah seems to be doing is quoting Peter's assertion that he is clever in circumstances which make it seem ridiculous, thereby mocking his assertion. Such an account can explain how we are able to interpret irony: we recognise an ironical utterance not as an assertion itself, but as a quotation and the context makes clear that the speaker disagrees with what is being quoted.

see also...

Metaphor; Pragmatics; Semantics

Jakobson, Roman

Roman Jakobson (1896–1983) was born and educated in Russia but later moved to Czechoslovakia. He was one of the founders of the Prague School of linguistics, which was strongly influenced by the ideas of Ferdinand de Saussure. Jakobson later emigrated to America, where he held professorial posts at Columbia and later Harvard. He published widely in the fields of linguistics, philology, literary theory and anthropology.

Jakobson's most important contribution to linguistics was the idea of a 'distinctive feature'. Humans are capable of making a wide range of sounds with their vocal apparatus (including coughs, grunts, burps and so on), but not all of these are made use of by language. Jakobson developed a theory to distinguish speech sounds from these other sounds. His proposal was that all the speech sounds of all languages are composed of a small number of 'distinctive features' such as nasal, labial and so on. All of these features were 'binary', meaning that they could only be marked as either present [+] or absent [–].

The idea of distinctive features was fundamental to subsequent developments in phonology, since it not only allowed a principled distinction to be drawn between speech sounds and non-speech sounds, but also provided the basis for the systematic classification of speech sounds into groups. Jakobson developed a similar style of analysis for morphology, which also proved to be influential.

see also...

Distinctive feature; Phoneme; Phonology; Saussure

Language

It is difficult to imagine what life would be like without language. Unlike any other species on earth, we can communicate with each other about almost anything, jot down reminder notes for ourselves, write our memoirs. People from the distant past can share their thoughts with us through books and we can likewise record ours for posterity. All this is made possible because of something special about the biological makeup of our brains, something that gives us the ability to acquire and use language.

Because all humans share basically the same biological make up, we all have the same ability to use language, and the languages that we employ all have a great many properties in common (called 'universals'). Apart from a few truly rare exceptions, all humans use language; most often this is a spoken language, but in some cases it is a sign language. Although the universal properties of language are part of our biology, the particular properties of our own language must be acquired as a child.

There is a widespread idea that human speech can be divided into separate languages and that these separate languages can be further subdivided into dialects. There is no clear linguistic basis for this idea, however. Whether we choose to call the speech of a group of people a language or a dialect is mainly a sociological or political decision rather than a linguistic one.

see also...

Acquisition of language; Dialect; Universal

Language and thought

Language and thought seem to be inextricably linked – we think in words and it is sometimes difficult to imagine how we could think without language. Some scholars have even questioned whether thought is *possible* without language.

The evidence suggests, however, that we do not need language in order to think. There are cases of people who have no language but whose thinking appears normal (mostly these are profoundly deaf children who have not been exposed to a sign language). Also, very young babies who have no language have nevertheless been shown to have fairly complex thoughts (e.g. they can do mental arithmetic and think about the movement of physical objects). In addition, there is even anecdotal evidence from artists and scientists that some of their most important thinking is done with mental images rather than words.

While we may not *need* language in order to think, perhaps language can *influence* how we think. Again, the evidence suggests not. The way we think about the world seems to be influenced mainly by perception rather than language. For example, some languages have words for only two colours ('light' and 'dark'), but speakers of these languages perceive and classify coloured objects in basically the same way as speakers of languages with more colour terms. Rather than language influencing thought, it seems that thought influences language and that universal aspects of thought are the reason for some of the universal aspects of language.

Some people also suggest that language is a product of our intelligence. This is almost certainly false, as there are cases of people with severe mental disability whose language is normal (e.g. Williams Syndrome), and of people with severe language defects but normal intelligence (e.g. aphasia).

see also...

Language disorders; Sapir–Whorf hypothesis

Language contact

Whenever speakers of one language interact with speakers of another language, the two languages are said to be in contact. Nearly all languages are in contact with some other language and this can be seen in the influence that the languages have on each other. These influences include the introduction of loan words, grammatical and phonological changes, as well as an increase in bilingualism.

Loan words are commonly introduced because they name new objects or ideas. It is natural to take on the foreign name for an object that has not been encountered before (this happened when speakers of English first encountered coffee and kangaroos, for example). It can also happen when a contact language has a particular prestige (this is the reason why so many French words found their way into English after the Norman Conquest).

Another process that may occur as a result of language contact is the development of pidgins. A pidgin is a simplified language created by people who have no language in common, in order to enable a crude form of communication to take place. Because no one speaks it as a native language, and because it does not have a real grammar, a pidgin is not really a language at all.

Language contact has always been common, but never more so than in the last few centuries, which have seen massive colonisation, a dramatic increase in international travel and the advent of rapid long-distance communication.

see also...

Bilingualism; Creoles and pidgins; Sociolinguistics

Language disorders

All people, regardless of their general level of intelligence, acquire language in the same way and at about the same speed. There are two ways in which language disorders can arise: through damage to the brain or through genetic defects. (Speech defects such as stuttering or lisping are not considered language disorders, since they are caused by problems with muscles or nerves controlling speech and do not result from problems with language itself.)

Language disorders that result from damage to the brain are known as 'aphasia'. There are also a number of genetic defects which can affect language, including 'Specific Language Impairment'. The symptoms of language disorders can vary widely, depending on which part of the brain is affected. Specific Language Impairment, as the name suggests, causes problems specifically with language (such as problems with morphology), but has few non-linguistic effects. Aphasia, on the other hand, can devastate language use completely or it can cause extremely specific problems. For example, there have been cases of patients who were unable to use or understand words for fruit and vegetables, but who had no problems with other words. Other patients have difficulty with verbs, but have no difficulty with nouns, even when the noun and the verb sound the same (so they would understand *a cover* but not *to cover*).

The fact that otherwise intelligent people can have severe language defects, and that people with very low IQs or other severe developmental problems can have normal language abilities, provides strong support for the idea that the acquisition and use of language does not depend on general intelligence or problem solving abilities, but on a specific 'language faculty' in the brain.

see also...

Acquisition of language;
Morphology; Psycholinguistics

Language family

Languages are constantly changing. And as groups of speakers become separated from each other, either geographically or politically, their languages begin to change in different ways. Over time, these changes become so great that we can no longer speak of a single language. Something like this happened when the Roman Empire began to break up. As various groups of speakers in different parts of the Empire lost contact with one another, the dialects of Latin which they spoke developed in different ways, and eventually gave rise to what we now call French, Italian, Spanish (and the other Romance languages). Latin itself (along with Ancient Greek, Sanskrit and others) is derived from an even older language called Proto-Indo-European, originally spoken in Central Asia around 4000 BCE. Languages that are derived from a common proto-language constitute a 'language family'.

By studying the similarities among languages in a family, linguists can learn a great deal about the parent language, even if no written records for this language exist. In this way, a number of language families and their proto-languages have been identified around the world. Some other languages are thought to be 'isolates' – that is, they are not related to any other language, presumably because they are the last surviving member of a language family. Some researchers try to go even further back in time, suggesting that some language families are derived from a single proto-proto-language. This is very difficult to prove and many linguists are sceptical of such claims. Some people even claim to have evidence for Proto-World, a single ancestor for all the world's languages, but these claims are generally dismissed.

see also...

Historical linguistics; Typology

Lexicon

You have almost certainly never before come across the sentence: *'Mars is inhabited by small, furry penguins'*. In fact, most of the sentences you come across every day you have never seen before and yet you have no difficulty in understanding them. The reason is that although there is an infinite number of sentences in any language, they are all constructed out of a finite set of words. And if we understand the words, as well as the grammar of the language, then we can understand an infinite number of sentences.

In order to do this, we must have a mental 'list' of all the words we know (around 60,000 for a well-educated speaker of English). This mental list is called our 'lexicon'. Several kinds of information about each word must be listed in the lexicon, such as its meaning, syntactic information (e.g. the fact that *foot* is a noun), morphological information (e.g. that *foot* has the irregular plural *feet*) and phonological information (e.g. that the pronunciation of *foot* is /fʊt/). Not all words need to be listed in the lexicon. For example, it is not necessary to list *rain*, *rains*, and *raining*. Only *rain* needs to be listed and the other forms can be derived from regular rules (which are also stored in the lexicon). Irregular forms (such as *feet*) need to be listed, since they cannot be derived by rules in the lexicon. Those words which need to be listed in the lexicon are known as 'lexical items'.

The term 'lexicon' is also sometimes used to refer to the set of words of a language (rather than just the words known by an individual speaker).

---

see also...

Grammar; Word

Logic and linguistics

The immortal words of the Rolling Stones – *'I can't get no satisfaction'* – have caused much consternation among the self-appointed guardians of the English language. It is often said that since, in logic, two negatives make a positive, what Mick Jagger is really saying is that he *can* get satisfaction. Dialects that make use of so-called 'double negatives' are often claimed by non-linguists to be 'illogical'. This view assumes that ideas from logic can be straightforwardly applied to language.

In fact, however, this is not the case. Logic is the study of abstract systems of reasoning developed by philosophers, whereas our ability to understand language is biologically evolved. There is no reason to assume that the two should be based on identical principles. For example, language uses the repetition of a word as a way of intensifying its meaning (as in **very very** *good*), and many languages, including English, use repeated negatives for the same purpose (*'No, no!'* doesn't mean 'yes'). Agreement is also common in language (e.g., a plural subject takes the plural form of a verb), and this is what we see in the sentence we started with: *no* is agreeing with the negated verb, just as the negative word *any* does in 'standard' dialects.

This is not to say that there is no relation between logic and linguistics, however. Linguists have used the tools of logic in semantics, in order to characterise some aspects of the meaning of language (including the meanings of words such as *and* and *or*).

see also...

Agreement; Semantics

Manner of articulation

Speech sounds are classified by linguists according to how they are produced. For consonants, there are two important factors: the *manner* in which they are produced ('manner of articulation') and *where* in the vocal tract they are made ('place of articulation'). It is also necessary to specify whether a consonant is 'voiced' (produced with vibrating vocal cords) or not. Other methods are used for classifying vowels.

Consonants are made by narrowing the vocal tract at some point, thereby restricting the flow of air. The place where this happens is the 'place of articulation', but it is also possible to narrow the vocal tract in different ways, called the 'manner of articulation'. For example, the vocal tract can be completely closed, then suddenly opened. Sounds made in this way are known as 'plosives' (e.g. [p] or [k]). If the vocal tract is instead opened gradually, we have an 'affricate' (e.g. the '*ch*' in *choose*). If a friction noise is made by forcing air through a narrow opening, we have a 'fricative' (e.g. [f]). When air is completely blocked from passing through the mouth, but is allowed to pass through the nose,

then we have a 'nasal' (e.g. [n] or [m]). The tongue can be made to rapidly vibrate, producing what is called a 'trill' (like the [r] in Spanish). It is also possible to make the tongue vibrate just once, in which case we have a 'flap'.

Languages also have sounds that are made through a fairly large opening, like vowels, but which behave as if they are consonants. These are known as 'approximants' (e.g. [w]).

---

see also...

Consonant; Phonetics; Place of articulation

Metaphor

We often use language in a non-literal way. Metaphors are an obvious example: when I say *'John is a pig'* I do not mean that John is a four-legged farm animal. Rather, I attribute certain stereotypical properties of pigs (such as slovenliness) to John. As well as using nouns metaphorically, we also use verbs (*'I see your point'*), as well as phrases, sentences and even whole texts. Metaphors are common in all languages, but how are we able to understand metaphorical utterances?

Metaphors assert that there are relevant connections between normally unrelated things (say, between John and a pig). It is then up to the hearer to work out what these connections are. Linguists and psychologists are increasingly regarding metaphor as a fundamental thought process and there is evidence that the basis of many metaphors is universal (for example, the idea that anger is heat, seen in metaphors such as *'You make my blood boil'* and *'Cool down!'*).

It is often claimed that we can recognise something as a metaphor by noticing that it is literally false. There are problems with this view, however. First, not all literally false utterances are metaphorical – ironical utterances such as *'Lovely weather!'* (uttered during a downpour) are also literally false, but when we hear such utterances, we would never try to interpret them as metaphorical. The second problem is that not all metaphors are literally false. If I say *'John is no pig'*, I am saying something which is literally true, but I would never be understood to be making the banal claim that John is not a kind of farm animal.

see also...

Irony; Pragmatics

Mood and modality

Languages modify verbs in various ways to express different distinctions. For example, verbs may indicate 'tense' (whether the activity expressed by the verb took place in the past, present or future, say) or 'aspect' (other temporal features of the activity, such as its duration, and whether the action is complete). Languages also modify verbs in order to express various attitudes, such as whether the activity was possible, certain or unlikely. This is known as 'mood'.

English does not have a well-developed mood system and we mostly use adverbs to express mood. For example, we can express various degrees of certainty using adverbs: *'It will rain'* versus *'It will possibly rain'*, *'It will probably rain'*, *'Maybe it will rain'*. Other languages might express such distinctions by modifying the verb. English retains a separate verb form for the 'subjunctive' mood, to express counterfactual situations (for example, *were* in *if I were you*), but it does so only in formal situations or fixed idiomatic expressions.

Some linguists make a distinction between 'mood' and 'modality'. They use the term 'modality' for the expression of obligation, permission, prohibition, necessity, possibility and ability. They reserve the term 'mood' for expression of reality (i.e. whether something is certain, uncertain, counterfactual and so on). It is very difficult, however, to draw a clear distinction between mood and modality.

see also...

Aspect; Tense; Verb

Morpheme

In the same way that sentences are made up of combinations of words, so words are made up of combinations of smaller units known as 'morphemes'. The word *unlikely*, for example, is made up of three morphemes: the 'prefix' *un-*, the 'stem' *like*, and the 'suffix' *-ly*. Each of these morphemes also occurs in other English words (e.g. *un-zip*, *dis-like*, *quick-ly*). Morphemes are the smallest elements of a language that have a distinct meaning.

Words may consist of just a single morpheme (e.g. *man*, *like*), in which case they are known as 'monomorphemic'. Words which are made up of more than one morpheme (e.g. *dis-like*, *un-help-ful-ness*) are known as 'polymorphemic'. Linguists often classify morphemes according to whether they are 'free' (able to occur as words in their own right, such as *like*), or 'bound' (not able to occur unless attached to another morpheme, such as *un-*, or *-ly*). Morphemes are sometimes also classified according to whether they have a 'grammatical' function (like *-ness*, which turns an adjective into a noun) or a 'lexical' function (they carry word meaning, like *man* or *help*).

A single morpheme may be pronounced differently in different words, such as the past tense morpheme in *slept* (/t/), *minded* (/id/) and *smiled* (/d/). In some cases it can be very difficult to decide how to split a word into morphemes. For example, *cats* contains two morphemes: the stem *cat* and the plural morpheme *-s*. Likewise, the word *feet* must also contain two morphemes: the stem *foot* and the plural morpheme, but these do not appear as separate parts of the word.

see also...

Lexicon; Morphology; Word

Morphology

Why is it that we can speak of a house as *mice infested* but not *rats-infested* – we have to say that it is *rat-infested*? Morphology is the branch of linguistics that studies questions such as this about the internal structure of words. There are two main branches: 'derivational morphology' and 'inflectional morphology'.

Derivational morphology deals with processes that change a word with one part of speech or meaning into a word with a different part of speech or meaning. For example, there is a regular derivational process in English which creates a noun from a verb by adding *-er* (so *walk* becomes *walker*). Another example is the process which adds *un-* to an adjective to derive another adjective of opposite meaning (so *like* becomes *unlike*).

Inflectional morphology, in contrast, deals with processes that alter the form of a word without changing either its part of speech or its meaning. An example is the regular *-s* inflection in English, which creates plural forms of nouns (so *rat* becomes *rats*).

It turns out that derivational processes always apply *before* inflectional processes. This answers our initial question, because compounding – the process which joins two words together to form a new word – is like a derivational process in that it must always occur before any inflectional processes. We cannot add the plural inflection *-s* to *rat* before we compound it with *infest*, so we cannot get *rats-infested*. *Mice*, however, is an irregular plural which is not formed by an inflectional process (it is just a separate word that we have to learn as the plural of *mouse*). We can thus form either *mouse-infested* or *mice-infested*.

see also...

Morpheme; Part of speech; Word

Motherese

There is a special form of speech reserved by adults for talking to infants. This is called 'motherese' or more generally 'caregiver speech'. It is distinguished by short, repetitive sentences: 'Look, there's a doggie! See the doggie? Say hello to the doggie! Nice doggie!' It also commonly contains special 'baby words' such as 'doggie', 'kitty' and 'choo-choo'. In addition, there are a high proportion of questions compared with adult language.

Motherese has a similar form across many different cultures. There are some cultures, however, where motherese is absent (for example, in Samoa). Because children in these cultures do not learn language any more slowly, we know that motherese is not necessary for children to learn language. So why is motherese so widespread?

It may just be that parents from many different cultures *think* that young children need to be spoken to in motherese. A better explanation, however, is that motherese has melodies that attract the child's attention and that can be interpreted by the child – for example, a rise-and-fall contour for approving and short, sharp bursts for prohibiting. These same patterns occur across languages and cultures and are possibly universal. Also, these melodies mark the sounds as speech and can also indicate sentence boundaries and new words. While this information may be useful to the child, it is clearly not vital.

see also...

Acquisition of language

Noun

Words such as *cat, oil* and *problem*, which traditional grammars defined as the 'name for a person, place, or thing', are members of the class of nouns. The problems with the traditional definition are immediately apparent. First, not all nouns seem to fit the definition (is a problem a thing?). Second, there are words like *red*, which names a colour, but which is most commonly used as an adjective rather than as a noun.

Linguists prefer to define nouns in terms of their grammatical properties. For example, nouns may follow prepositions (as in *with **glee***), may occur with determiners (as in *that **cat***), and may be modified by adjectives (as in *difficult **problem***). Nouns may change their form to indicate their case (depending on whether they are subjects, objects and so on), their number (whether they are singular or plural, for example) or their gender (whether they are masculine or feminine, for example). The ways in which nouns indicate these categories vary from language to language.

A distinction is often made between count nouns and non-count nouns.

Count nouns are those that denote separate entities, so we can have *a cat, three cats* or *few cats*, for example. Non-count nouns denote continuous entities – we cannot have **an oil* or **few oil*, but must instead use *some oil* or *little oil*.

Another distinction that is often made is between proper nouns and common nouns. Proper nouns denote individuals, such as *Isaac Newton* or *Dublin*, which cannot be used with articles we cannot say (**the Dublin*). Common nouns, such as *person* or *city*, do not denote particular individuals.

see also...

Case; Gender; Grammatical category; Morphology; Number; Part of speech

Number

All languages have a variety of words referring to numbers of things: *one*, *two*, *many*, *few*, *six-point-three*, *half*, *two million*. Many languages also make grammatical distinctions between different numbers of things. For example, in English most nouns come in two forms, depending on whether we wish to refer to just one thing, or many of them: *dog* and *dogs*, *child* and *children*, *foot* and *feet* (but there are a few exceptions like *sheep*). English pronouns show a similar contrast: *I* versus *we* and *he/she/it* versus *they*. English is thus said to have two 'numbers' – 'singular' and 'plural'.

Some languages do not indicate number grammatically at all, whereas other languages have more than two numbers. Sanskrit, for example, had three numbers, corresponding to singular, dual (two things) and plural. Other languages with three numbers have a slightly different system: they have different forms for one thing (singular), a few things ('paucal') and many things (plural). Fijian has four numbers for pronouns: singular ('I'), dual ('we two'), trial ('we three') and plural.

It is important to note that, as with many other grammatical notions, number does not correspond exactly to the number of objects referred to. For example, nouns which appear to be singular may refer to more than one object (as in the English sentence *'The board have decided to accept the proposal'*, where *board* is singular, but takes *have*, the plural form of the verb). Conversely, some nouns such as *scissors* appear to be plural, but can refer to a single object.

see also...

Grammatical category; Noun;
Pronoun and proform

Object

In traditional grammars, the object was seen as the 'goal' or 'recipient' of an action (as in *'Monty Python killed **the parrot**'*, where the parrot is the unfortunate recipient of the action of killing). The problem with such an approach is that in sentences such as *'John is easy to please'*, the subject *John* is the recipient of the pleasing, but appears in subject position. Sentences such as *'The athlete set a world record'* are also problematic, since *a world record* did not in any sense 'receive' the action of setting, as the record did not exist before the setting took place. Linguists prefer to define objects syntactically, in terms of the structural position they occupy in the sentence (or clause).

A distinction is often made between 'direct objects' (usually just called 'objects') and 'indirect objects'. Indirect objects typically *do* refer to the recipient of an action (direct objects often do not, as we have seen). In English, the indirect object must either precede the direct object or it must be marked with a preposition (such as *to*). For example, in the sentence *'They offered John a car'*, the indirect object is *John* (who gets the car), and *the car* is the direct object. We can also say *'They offered a car to John'*. Because in this case the indirect object *John* follows the direct object, it must be marked with the preposition *to*. Other languages use case markings rather than prepositions to mark direct and indirect objects.

see also...

Agent and patient; Case; Subject

Origin of language

little is known about how and when human language came into existence, although there is a great deal of speculation. Certain proposals can be safely ruled out, however. First, language is not merely a cultural innovation: no culture has ever been found that lacked language and children who grow up in an environment without language (e.g. some deaf children, or children exposed to a pidgin) will create one. Studies from historical linguistics also suggest that language probably arose in several places independently. Similarly, it is unlikely that language arose as a by-product of our general intelligence – language has a specific biological basis and there are cases of people with normal intelligence who cannot learn language, as well as people with impaired intelligence who have no problems with language.

Given that it is so completely different from other systems of animal communication, including those of the apes, most researchers believe that language did not result merely from enhancements in capacities we share with non-human primates. Instead, it is likely that language evolved in our human ancestors. Whether it evolved as an adaptation for communication or as a by-product of brain mechanisms involved in other capacities such as tool use, social skills or symbolic thought, however, is hotly debated.

Estimates of when language arose differ markedly. On one view language arose with the advent of modern *Homo sapiens*, around 100,000 years ago. Another popular view locates the birth of language at the time of the 'cultural explosion' around 40,000 years ago. Some anthropologists, however, claim to have evidence for language areas in the brains of hominids from 1–2 million years ago.

see also...

Acquisition of language; Animal communication; Creoles and pidgins; Language disorders

Part of speech (word class)

This is a traditional term used by grammarians to refer to different classes of words such as nouns, pronouns, verbs, adjectives and so on. In traditional grammars, these terms were not defined in a clear or systematic way. For example, verbs are often said to denote actions, but there are plenty of verbs that do not denote actions (e.g. the verb *seem*) and there are lots of words that denote actions without being verbs (e.g. the noun *destruction*).

Linguists try to define word classes in a precise way, on the basis of grammatical properties. For example, nouns can be plural or singular, can have case and can follow an article such as *the*. A word is a noun, or a verb, because of the grammatical rules it obeys, not because of anything about its meaning, in rather the same way as a chess piece is defined by the moves it makes, rather than its shape or colour.

The word classes may be divided into two kinds: *open classes* and *closed classes*. Open classes are those word classes whose membership is unlimited and to which new items may be freely added. This is true, for example, of nouns: if we invent a novel kind of object, we can easily invent a new noun to name it. It is very difficult, however, to add a new determiner (like *a* or *the*) and so the class of determiners is said to be closed.

see also...

Adjective; Adverb and adverbial; Determiner; Grammatical cateogry; Noun; Preposition and postposition; Verb

Person

Languages generally make a distinction between three different roles in speech: the speaker (or a group including the speaker), the person or group spoken to and the person or thing spoken about. Linguists refer to these as the 'first person' (*I*, *we*), the 'second person' (*you*), and the 'third person' (*he*, *she*, *it*, *they*). Person is usually marked on pronouns, and/or on verbs. In English, the different pronouns mark not only person, but also number (singular or plural, as in *I* versus *we*), gender (as in *she* versus *he*), and animacy (*she* or *he* versus *it*).

The three-way contrast of person appears to be common to all languages, but there are nevertheless certain differences between languages in their use of the contrast. Some languages, for example, have different first-person plural (*we*) forms, depending on whether or not it includes the person or group spoken to. These are known as 'inclusive' and 'exclusive' forms. English does not make this distinction, so in a sentence such as *'Shall we go now?'*, the pronoun *we* could refer to a group of people including the addressee(s), or to a group of people excluding the addressee(s).

Some languages also make a distinction between 'formal' and 'informal' pronouns (for example, French *vous* and *tu*). A few languages (mostly in North America) have two separate third-person forms, one for the person or thing currently being talked about (the 'proximate') and one for a person or thing mentioned in passing (the 'obviative').

see also...

Grammatical category; Pronoun and proform

Phoneme

Consider the letter 'p'. I can write it in many different ways: *p*, **p**, P, *p*, or even ℙ, but it is still the same letter. I cannot rotate it, however, or it becomes the letter 'd'. Similarly, I can say the sound /p/ in many different ways: loudly, softly, huskily (when I have a cold), with a puff of air (as in the word *pin*), without a puff of air (as in the word *spin*) and so on, but it is still the /p/ sound. This is because the language ignores changes in loudness, huskiness and so on, so these do not create a different sound. The different sounds of a language are known as 'phonemes'.

The reason languages ignore some changes in pronunciation is that speech sounds are actually made up of smaller units known as 'distinctive features'. We can only change a sound by changing one of these features. For example, the phoneme /n/ is composed of the features [+nasal] (air passes through the nose), [−continuant] (air is blocked from passing through the mouth) and [+coronal] (tongue tip is elevated). Since there is no feature for loudness, I cannot change the speech sound by saying it louder. If I change /n/ to [−nasal], however, I make a different sound, /d/.

English has about 40 phonemes (depending on the dialect), which is about average. The Brazilian language Pirahã has only ten phonemes (the smallest number of any known language), while the African language !Xũ has 141 phonemes.

see also...

Distinctive feature; Phonology

Phonetics

Phonetics is the scientific study of human speech sounds. It aims to develop a systematic method for describing and classifying these sounds. All aspects of a sound are investigated, including how it is made by the vocal organs ('articulatory phonetics'), the physical properties of the sound wave itself ('acoustic phonetics') and how it is perceived by the ear and brain ('auditory phonetics').

The description and classification of speech sounds makes use of terms from related disciplines such as anatomy and acoustics. For example, speech sounds may be classified according to their place of articulation (whether they are made with the tongue touching the teeth or the roof of the mouth, say), or their acoustic properties (the frequency and intensity of the sound waves). They may also be classified according to how they are perceived – for example in terms of the 'pitch' we hear a sound as having (this is related to the frequency of the sound wave) or its 'loudness' (a property which depends in part on the intensity of the sound wave, but which can also be affected by the wave's frequency).

Because phonetics investigates the properties of sounds themselves, rather than how these sounds are made use of by language, phonetics is not strictly speaking a branch of linguistics. Phonetics is, however, fundamental to much work in linguistics and there is some degree of overlap between phonetics and phonology.

see also...

Phoneme; Phonology

Phonology

Just as in English we use an alphabet of 26 letters to write down the words of our language, so too in our minds we have a set of basic sound units (such as /p/, /b/, and /o/) that we put together in different ways to form spoken words. These basic units of sound are known as 'phonemes'. English makes use of around 40 different phonemes (depending on the dialect); some languages use as few as ten, and some more than 100.

The area of linguistics that studies the sound systems of languages is known as 'phonology'. The human speech organs are capable of making a wide variety of sounds (including burps, coughs and whistles), but only a fraction of these possible sounds are used in language. Phonologists try to explain why languages make use of some sounds and not others and investigate the ways in which the sound systems of languages are organised. They also devise rules to explain why phonemes are not always pronounced in the same way – for example, /p/ is pronounced [p] in *spin*, but [p^h] (with an extra puff of air) in *pin*.

One important finding is that phonemes can be split into smaller units known as 'distinctive features'. This allows linguists to systematically classify phonemes. In addition to phonemes and distinctive features, phonologists also study 'suprasegmental' features of language such as 'stress', 'tone' and 'intonation'. These features convey important linguistic information, but they are not properties of individual phonemes. Rather, they are properties of larger units of sound such as syllables or words.

see also...

Distinctive feature; Intonation; Phoneme; Phonetics

Phrase

In order to form sentences, words are first combined into larger structures called phrases, according to principles laid down in the grammar of the language. For example, we might start with a noun such as *dogs* and build up a phrase such as *fierce dogs*, or *fierce black dogs*, or even *fierce black dogs with sharp teeth*. In each case, because we have started with a noun, the phrase will be a 'noun phrase'. A phrase such as *eats very quickly indeed* is built up around the verb *eats* and so is a 'verb phrase'. There are phrases corresponding to all parts of speech (e.g. preposition phrases such as *right over to the left*, and adjective phrases such as *very happy indeed*). The word around which a phrase is constructed, and from which the phrase gets its name, is know as the 'head'. Every phrase must have a head.

The simplest phrases are single words. For example, in the sentence *'Cats are furry'*, the subject (*cats*) is both a noun and a complete noun phrase (so we can replace it with another noun phrase, such as *fierce domestic cats*, to form the sentence *'Fierce domestic cats are furry'*). Other phrases can be very complex, for example the noun phrase *'those old red shoes which my mother used to wear on summer evenings as a young girl'*.

see also...

Head; Part of speech

Place of articulation

We classify speech sounds according to how they are produced. There are two important factors in classifying consonants: where in the vocal tract they are made ('place of articulation') and the manner in which they are produced ('manner of articulation'). It is also necessary to specify whether a consonant is 'voiced' (produced with vibrating vocal cords) or not. Other methods are used for classifying vowels.

The different places of articulation for consonants are named using anatomical labels, so we have: 'labial' (for sounds made with the lips), 'dental' (the teeth), 'alveolar' (the ridge behind the top front teeth), 'palatal' (the palate, or roof of the mouth), 'velar' (the velum, or soft palate at the back of the mouth), 'uvular' (the back of the throat) 'pharyngeal' (the pharynx, lower in the throat), and 'glottal' (the glottis, or larynx).

Try saying the sound [t]. Notice that as you say it, your tongue touches the ridge behind your front teeth, so [t] is an alveolar consonant. Now say the sound [f]. This is made with the lower lip touching the teeth, so we need to identify both these articulators: we call [f] a labio-dental consonant. In cases like this, the lower articulator always comes first in the label.

Not all languages use all places of articulation. For example, standard English does not make use of any uvular or pharyngeal sounds.

---

see also...

Consonant; Manner of articulation; Phonetics

Politeness

Human cultures tend to place great importance on politeness. In general, we try not to offend others and we expect others not to offend us. Of course, what we consider to be offensive varies from culture to culture. Politeness is also an important factor governing our use of language.

Sociolinguists have studied politeness in great detail in recent years. There are a number of ways in which the cultural rules governing politeness affect language. Politeness may affect tone of voice, the use of politeness indicators (such as *please*), whether we use direct or indirect questions and even whether we choose to speak at all. In many languages, the expression of politeness has even been encoded in the grammar. For example, Javanese has five different levels of politeness, depending on who is being addressed, how formal the conversation is and how respectful the speaker wishes to be. These different levels are indicated by the use of different pronouns and also different nouns and verbs.

Politeness can also be used to explain how we structure conversations. For example, we periodically pause and allow others to take turns in the conversation and we do not end a conversation without first offering others a chance to say something further (so we typically use a pre-closing remark such as *'Well, I'd better be going now…'* before actually ending a conversation).

see also...

Sociolinguistics

Pragmatics

Pragmatics is the study of how utterances are interpreted in context. This is in contrast to semantics, which is the study of those aspects of meaning which are independent of context. For example, consider the sentence *'John is overweight'*. Semantics (together with other parts of the grammar) will be able to give some general indication of the meaning of this sentence, but it will not be able to determine what an utterance of this sentence means in a given context. Thus, while the grammar will give a general meaning for *overweight* and specify that *John* refers to someone (or something) called 'John', it will have nothing to say about which individual the speaker was referring to, or the precise sense in which he is *overweight* (this would depend, for example, on whether John was a sumo wrestler or a jockey).

In order to interpret the meaning of a particular utterance, it is necessary to use non-linguistic information (such as who the speaker happened to be looking at) as well as linguistic information. It is possible to formulate pragmatic rules to explain how people interpret certain aspects of utterances

(for example, a simple rule can be used to interpret *I*, along the lines of '*I* refers to the speaker of the utterance'), but a large part of utterance interpretation must involve more complex processes, since there is in principle no limit to the amount of contextual information that might be relevant in interpreting an utterance. These processes are thought to be inferential rather than rule governed.

see also...

Grice; Semantics; Utterance

Preposition and postposition

Words such as *in, to* and *of* are members of the class of prepositions. They are known as *pre*positions because they precede the phrase they combine with (as in **to** *the theatre*). They usually indicate a relationship between two or more entities, typically position or direction (as in *John went* **to** *the theatre* or *Teresa is standing* **between** *John and Emma*).

In English, many prepositions (but no other words) can be intensified by *right* or *straight* (e.g. *go* **straight** *to school*, **right** *up the top*). This criterion can only be used for the standard dialect of English, however. (In other dialects of English, *right* can modify other words, as in northern English expressions such as *right happy*.)

Instead of prepositions, many languages use *post*positions, which follow the phrase they combine with (so in Japanese we find *Tōkyō* **e**, which means 'to Tokyo'). The term 'adposition' is used as a general term for both prepositions and postpositions. Some languages use case endings on nouns where English would use a preposition (e.g. in Sanskrit *vane* means '**in** the forest').

Although most prepositions combine with noun phrases, they may also combine with preposition phrases (as in **over** *to the house*, where the preposition *over* is combined with the preposition phrase *to the house*), clauses (as in **since** *John is away*) or stand alone (as in *I've been there* **before**). In traditional grammars, prepositions which stood alone were called 'particles' and prepositions which combined with clauses were called 'conjunctions'.

see also...

Case; Clause; Noun; Part of speech; Phrase

Pronoun and proform

Words such as *he, them* and *nobody* are members of the class of pronouns. In traditional grammars they were often said to 'stand in for nouns', but in fact this is not very accurate. In reply to the question *'What nationality is the current Wimbledon champion?'* one might reply *'He is American'*. Here, the pronoun *he* is not standing in for a noun, but for the entire noun phrase *the current Wimbledon champion. He* cannot stand in for just the noun *champion*, as we can see from the absurdity of **'The current Wimbledon he is American'*.

There are many different types of pronoun, including 'personal pronouns' (*I, you, they*), 'possessive pronouns' (*my, its*), 'demonstrative pronouns' (*this, that*), 'reflexive pronouns' (*herself*), 'reciprocal pronouns' (*each other*) and 'relative pronouns' (*who*).

Although not usually recognised in traditional grammars, there are also words that stand in for other phrases. These words are known by the general term 'proform' (which also includes pronouns). For example, *there* stands in for preposition phrases (as in *I like to go to the Latin Quarter, but she doesn't like to go **there**); do* stands in for verb phrases (as in *I like chickens and they **do** too*); and *so* stands in for adjective phrases or whole clauses (as in *I don't think **so***).

see also...

Part of speech; Phrase

Psycholinguistics

This is the branch of linguistics that investigates the psychological processes associated with language. For example, when linguists investigate how children acquire language, they are developing a theory of a psychological process. In addition to language acquisition, psycholinguistics also investigates the processes involved in producing and comprehending language.

There are several different levels involved in the production and comprehension of language. The basic level is that of the sounds and gestures of language and psycholinguists investigate how these are produced, perceived and identified. The next level involves words (and signs, in the case of sign languages), as well as the structured arrangement of these words (their syntax and semantics). At this level, psycholinguists investigate sentence processing: how speakers formulate utterances and how listeners understand them. The next level involves the act of communication itself (i.e. pragmatics). Here, the emphasis is on investigating what speakers do with their utterances and how listeners understand what the speaker intended to communicate. The top level is that of discourse, which is the wider context of the activity within which language use is occurring.

Psycholinguists tend to study psychological processes involved in the language of 'normal' individuals (i.e. those without brain damage). A great deal of information can be gleaned, however, from studies of people with language disorders. These studies tend to be carried out in the field of neurolinguistics, which investigates the neurological basis for language (i.e. the areas of the brain involved in various aspects of language, and the effects of damage to these areas).

see also...

Acquisition of language; Language and thought; Language disorders

Register

We speak differently in different social situations. When we write a letter applying for a job, we would use very different language compared to when we write a letter to a close friend, and we do not speak to a teacher in the same way that we speak to a parent. From a young age, people learn to use different forms of language in different situations.

Many of the differences involve vocabulary. For example, we might use the word *pissed* in informal situations, *drunk* in somewhat more formal ones and *intoxicated* to a judge. Registers can also differ in many other ways, including syntax. For example, the English register of instructions (as found in recipes and on packaging) can omit objects: we find sentences such as *'Keep out of the reach of children'*, which would normally be understood as an exhortation to the reader to avoid children, but is understood in these situations to be advice on where to store the product (i.e. it is *'Keep this bottle out of the reach of children'*, with the object *this bottle* omitted). We are able to switch registers without thinking about it, which is why no one finds sentences like this odd.

In multilingual communities, it is common for different *languages* to be used in different social situations (for example, one language might be used in the home and another at school). In such cases the different languages are being used in the same way as registers.

see also...

Dialect; Language

Sapir–Whorf hypothesis

This is the theory, first put forward by anthropologist Edward Sapir and amateur linguist Benjamin Lee Whorf, that the way a person thinks is determined by the structure of their language. The theory is also known as 'linguistic determinism' or 'linguistic relativity'.

One of Whorf's examples was the fact that Eskimos have a large number of words for snow. He took this to indicate that speakers of Eskimos have a radically different way of thinking about the world than do speakers of English, say. But apart from the fact that Whorf's claims about Eskimo are false (English has about the same number of words relating to snow: *snow, slush, sleet, blizzard, avalanche*, etc.), the theory is clearly wrong. It would imply that accurate translation between languages was impossible, which it is not. It would also imply that it is necessary to have a word for something before one could think about it, but if this was true children could never learn any words at all. Also, as one linguist pointed out, interior decorators have many words for different shades of mauve, but we would not want to conclude that they have a radically different world-view from other people.

A weaker form of the Sapir–Whorf hypothesis states merely that the language we speak influences the way we think. This is certainly true in some sense, but it is relatively uninteresting. In fact, it would be very surprising if it were not true.

see also...

Language and thought

76

Saussure, Ferdinand de

Ferdinand de Saussure (1857–1913) was Professor of General Linguistics at the University of Geneva. He was dissatisfied with the way linguistics was then practised and was one of the first to try and set out a systematic framework for the study of language. He is now widely regarded as the father of modern linguistics. His major work is *Cours de linguistique générale* ('Course in general linguistics'), which was published posthumously in 1916 and is based on his lecture notes and other materials.

Saussure introduced a number of fundamental distinctions. He regarded the abstract language system shared by a community of speakers (what he called 'langue') as being distinct from the actual speech produced by those speakers (what he called 'parole'). This is somewhat similar to Chomsky's later distinction between competence and performance. He also saw two different ways in which a language could be described and analysed, either 'synchronically', taking a snapshot of the language at a specific moment in time and analysing its properties, or 'diachronically', looking at the changes in a language over time.

Another important distinction introduced by Saussure was between 'syntagmatic' and 'paradigmatic' relationships. Consider the sentence *'I will eat'*. This sentence consists of a sequence of three elements, each of which contributes something to the meaning of the whole. The relationship between these elements is known as syntagmatic. Each of the elements is also related to other similar elements which could replace it in the sentence. For example, *will* could be replaced by *shall* or *might*. The relationship between these elements is known as paradigmatic. Overall, Saussure conceived of language as a vast network of interrelated entities.

see also...

Chomsky; Competence and performance

Semantics

Semantics is the study of the meaning of language. There are two types of meaning: the meaning of language itself and the meaning which language has when used in a particular context. For example, consider the sentence *'Sarah is feeling unwell'*. This sentence means that Sarah is not feeling well. But it would communicate something different when uttered in response to the question *'Is Sarah coming to the party tonight?'* (it would mean something like 'Sarah is not coming to the party') from when it was uttered in response to the question *'Is Sarah going to miss work today?'* (in which case it would communicate something like 'Sarah is going to miss work today'). Linguists therefore distinguish between what a sentence means ('linguistic meaning') and what an utterance of that sentence communicates in a given context ('speaker meaning'). Semantics is the study of linguistic meaning (speaker meaning is studied in pragmatics).

Language has several properties which a theory of semantics must explain. One important property is that language is infinite, so we are able to understand an unlimited number of sentences, most of which we have never encountered before (e.g. you have no problem understanding *'My pet lobster ate three M&Ms today'*).

There are many different approaches to semantics. One of the most influential is 'truth-conditional semantics', which tries to reduce meaning to truth and falsehood. The idea is that in order to know what a sentence means, we need to know what things would have to be like in order for the sentence to be true.

see also...

Grice; Pragmatics; Utterance

Sentence

There are grammatical rules about how words may be combined to form phrases and grammatical rules about how phrases may be combined to form sentences. But there are no grammatical rules about how to combine sentences to form larger chunks of language. The sentence, then, is the largest grammatical unit in language. This does not mean that there are no rules at all governing how sentences may be combined – clearly there are. It merely means that any such rules are not contained within the grammar, but are rather the result of other kinds of mental process.

For linguists, then, sentences are abstract objects that are constructed by the grammar of a language. A sentence does not have to be something which people might actually say. As Chomsky pointed out, even the sentence *'Colourless green ideas sleep furiously'*, which is totally meaningless, is a grammatical sentence of English (whereas * *'Colourless sleep furiously ideas green'* is not).

Linguists often classify sentences into different types, according to their grammatical properties. Typical sentence types include 'declaratives' (which are usually used to make statements), 'interrogatives' (which are usually used to ask questions), 'imperatives' (which are usually used to give commands) and 'exclamatives' (which, as you've probably guessed, are usually used to make exclamations).

see also...

Chomsky; Clause; Grammar; Utterance

Sign languages

It used to be thought that all human languages were spoken languages and that sign languages were merely crude gestural codes. But this is not the case. Detailed studies of sign languages show that they can be every bit as complex as spoken languages. There is an important distinction, however, between natural and non-natural sign languages.

Natural sign languages are those which have arisen spontaneously, and are used by people as a primary communications system. Except for the fact that they are signed rather than spoken, they are just like any other human language. Non-natural sign languages are those which have been intentionally invented (typically by educators of the deaf). They tend to violate universal principles of natural language and as a result are not readily acquired by children or widely adopted by deaf communities.

Natural sign languages appear to be as different from one another as spoken languages and they are not based on any spoken language. As with spoken languages, it is necessary to acquire a sign language as a child in order to have native fluency.

Acquisition proceeds similarly to spoken language, with the first signs appearing around age one, and two-sign sentences appearing in the second year.

American Sign Language (ASL) has been studied in the most detail. Word structure is very complex, with verbs marked for aspect, as well as agreement in person and number with both subject and object. As with other languages having a complex morphology (e.g. Latin), word order is relatively free. Studies of sign languages have confirmed that the human abilities for the acquisition and use of language are not specifically tied to speech.

> ### see also...
> *Agreement; Aspect; Case; Morphology; Word order*

Sociolinguistics

Different social groups use language in different ways and everyone uses language differently in different social situations. For example, accountants speak differently from physicists and we all speak differently when we are talking to family members than when we are talking to strangers. Sociolinguistics is the branch of linguistics that studies these relationships between language and society.

Among the areas investigated by sociolinguists are the social aspects of language contact, regional variations in language ('dialects'), variations in language between different social groups ('sociolects'), the different varieties of language used by the same person in different situations ('registers'), the different use of language between men and women ('gender differences') and the sometimes subtle differences in language use between individuals ('idiolects').

Because of these differences in the language used by different social groups, language has an important role in identifying speakers as members of a particular group. Every time we speak, we give other people clues as to which social groups we belong to, where we come from, and so on. Similarly, speaking Irish, or Basque, or another traditional language can be a public statement of individual identity and in some cases a powerful political statement, underlining rights to freedom or self-determination.

see also...

Dialect; Register

Speech act

As well as what we accomplish every day through physical acts such as eating, cleaning, cooking, carrying, driving and so on, we also accomplish a great deal through language. We perform linguistic actions, or 'speech acts', of different kinds in conversations, letters and emails. Language can be used to resign from a job, establish a legally binding contract, compliment someone, name a baby, grant a divorce and so on.

Speech acts may be of various kinds: 'directives' (commanding, requesting, etc.), 'declarations' (which bring about states of affairs, e.g. blessing, firing, arresting, convicting), 'commissives' (which commit a speaker to a course of action, e.g. promising, threatening, vowing), 'representatives' (asserting, claiming, or making other statements which may be true or false) and 'expressives' (greeting, apologising, thanking). The act performed by a speaker in uttering a sentence is known as the 'illocution'.

Recognising which speech act the speaker is attempting to perform can be vital to understanding utterances. An utterance such as *'You're leaving'* would be interpreted very differently depending on whether the speaker were issuing a command, expressing regret at the hearer's decision to leave, or asking a question. While the grammatical structure of a sentence and its intonation often provide clues as to the intended speech act, these are not always reliable. Determining the speech act of an utterance is thus a pragmatic process.

see also...

Pragmatics; Utterance

Stress

Syllables may be stressed or unstressed. Stressed syllables are more prominent, usually because they are louder (and sometimes also because they are longer or higher in pitch). Stress operates at both the word level ('lexical stress') and the sentence level ('sentence stress').

In some languages, such as English, lexical stress is not predictable – when we learn a word, we must also learn which of its syllables is stressed. For example, the first syllable of ˈphotograph is stressed, but the second syllable of deˈcision. Because of this, stress may be used in English to distinguish different words. For example, English has many words such as *record* and *import* that can be either nouns or verbs, depending on whether the stress is on the first or second syllable (thus we have the noun ˈrecord and the verb reˈcord). In other languages, however, lexical stress is predictable. For example, in French the lexical stress always falls on the last syllable (as in *monsieur*, *mademoiselle* or *au revoir*).

Sentence stress is used to emphasise certain parts of a sentence (e.g. *'I will NEver accept those terms'*). Sentence stress is usually placed on the syllable that normally bears lexical stress. Occasionally, however, sentence stress can be placed on a syllable which would not normally receive lexical stress (as in *'Pooh AND Piglet climbed the tree'*). This is sometimes known as 'contrastive stress'.

see also...

Syllable

Subject

In traditional grammars, sentences were divided into two parts: the subject and the predicate. The subject was traditionally seen as being the 'doer' (or 'agent') of the action expressed by the predicate. In other grammars the subject was seen as the 'topic' of the sentence (i.e. what the sentence is about). Linguists, however, have tended to emphasise how complex the notion of subject actually is.

One difficulty with the traditional approach is that there are many cases where the subject of a sentence is not an agent (e.g. '**John** appears unhappy' or '**That the Earth is flat** is obvious'), and also many cases where the agent is not the subject (e.g. in passive sentences such as 'The man was bitten by the dog', where it is the dog that is doing the biting, but *the man* is the subject). There are also many sentences where the subject is not a topic (e.g. '**It** is raining').

Linguists prefer to define subjects syntactically, using criteria such as where a phrase occurs in the structure of a sentence (or clause). In the sentence 'The man was bitten by the dog', the phrase *the man* is the subject because it occurs in subject position, despite the fact that it is the dog that is doing the biting. The term 'grammatical subject' is used for the phrase which occurs in subject position, to distinguish it from the 'logical subject', which in this case would be the phrase *the dog*.

see also...

Agent and patient; Case; Object

84

Syllable

Everyone knows that words can be divided into syllables – we say things like *'He doesn't understand words of more than one syllable'*, and speakers generally agree on how many syllables a given word has. Some languages have writing systems where a separate symbol is used for each syllable. Despite the fact that the notion seems to be a basic one in linguistics, however, linguists have found it remarkably difficult to give a precise definition of the syllable.

Phonetic definitions have included the 'pulse' theory, which argues that air is released from the lungs in a series of chest pulses and that each one of these pulses corresponds to a syllable. An alternative 'prominence' theory argues that some sounds are perceived to be louder (or more 'sonorous') than others and that peaks in sonority correspond to the centre of syllables. Neither of these theories has proved to be very successful, however.

Phonological theories, which look at the structure of syllables, have been more successful. Languages differ in which sequences of sounds they allow a syllable to have. Some languages only allow syllables consisting either of just a vowel (V), or a consonant followed by a vowel (CV). Other languages allow more complex syllables. The rules governing how the syllables of a language may be formed are known as 'phonotactic constraints'. These constraints can be used to give a definition of 'syllable' for a particular language.

see also...

Phonetics; Phonology; Writing system

Syntax

There is more to the meaning of a sentence that just the meanings of its words. For example, it is quite clear that the sentence *'Dogs chase cats'* means something quite different from the sentence *'Cats chase dogs'*, even though they contain exactly the same words. The point is that sentences are not just sequences of words – they have a certain *structure* and this affects their meaning. The study of sentence structure is known as 'syntax'.

The study of syntax was revolutionised in the 1950s by the linguist Noam Chomsky, who proposed a radical new theory known as transformational–generative grammar. Chomsky's aim was to develop a scientifically rigorous and psychologically plausible account of syntax. Chomsky's seminal work led to a flurry of research and to a number of different theories of syntax being proposed.

Sentences have a hierarchical structure, with words combining to form phrases and phrases combining to form clauses. A sentence consists of a single clause or a combination of clauses. Linguists often represent this structure in the form of a tree diagram. A remarkable discovery has been that syntax is largely similar across languages. Even languages that have been invented from scratch (either by deaf children, or by children raised hearing only a pidgin) show this same structure. The conclusion many linguists have reached is that the basic principles of syntax are innate and that individual languages can only differ in a certain limited number of ways (for example, in their basic word order).

see also...

Chomsky; Grammar; Transformational– generative grammar; Tree diagram; Word order

Tense

anguage and time are intimately connected and languages have a variety of ways of expressing temporal notions. The most obvious way is by using words which explicitly refer to time: *now, yesterday, next week, in a million years*. Many languages also express time grammatically, by changing the form of the verb. This is known as 'tense'. For example, English verbs have separate forms for 'past' and 'non-past' (which includes present and future), such as *go–went*, or *sleep–slept*. English has no future tense, but must instead resort to various expressions such as *will, be going to*, or *might* to express future time.

Other languages make a distinction between 'future' and 'non-future' tense, while yet others make more tense distinctions (languages with three, four or five tenses are not uncommon). Some languages, such as Chinese, do not use tense at all. Even in those languages which do mark tense, its relationship with time is often not direct – for example, the English present tense may be used to refer to past events in certain contexts (as in: *'Yesterday, I'm on my way to work as usual, when suddenly…'*). Tense is closely related to another grammatical property of verbs, namely 'aspect'. Whereas tense is concerned with a location in time (such as past, present or future), aspect refers to other temporal properties such as how long an event lasts, whether it is complete or incomplete and so on. It can often be difficult to draw a clear distinction between tense and aspect, so some linguists prefer to work with a single notion of tense-aspect.

see also...
Aspect; Mood; Verb

Tone and tone language

When a syllable is uttered it has a certain pitch (or frequency). In some languages (including many in Africa and South East Asia) changes in pitch are used to change the meanings of words. When pitch affects word meaning or provides grammatical information about a word (such as its tense), the pitch is referred to as a 'tone'. Languages which change the meanings of words in this way are known as 'tone languages'. Thai, for example, has five tones: high, mid, low, falling, and rising. The syllable *mai* can mean 'not', 'new', 'wood', 'burn' or 'does it?', depending on its tone. We could even construct the Thai sentence *'Mai mai mai mai mai'*, which when pronounced with the correct tones means 'New wood doesn't burn, does it?'

Tone languages have various numbers of tones. The West African language Hausa has two tones (high and low), the Beijing dialect of Chinese has four tones and the Cantonese dialect of Chinese has nine tones.

Tones with a fixed pitch are called 'level tones', and those with a varying pitch (such as falling, or rising–falling) are called 'contour tones'.

English is not a tone language. Rather than using pitch to change word meaning, English uses patterns of pitch to indicate something about the whole utterance (for example, English questions have a rising pitch at the end, statements have a falling pitch, and exclamations have rising–then–falling pitch). These pitch patterns are known as intonation, and languages such as English are known as 'intonation languages'. Tone languages also make use of intonation, but usually in a more limited way.

see also...
Intonation; Syllable

Topic

The topic of a sentence is 'what the sentence is about'. For example, the topic of the sentence *'John has been working hard all day'* is *John*, since this sentence says something about John. Often, the topic of a sentence corresponds to the grammatical subject, as in the previous example. This need not be the case, however, and we find sentences such as *'The exam I found very difficult'*, where *the exam* is the topic but not the subject. The topic of a sentence corresponds to 'old' information (that is, information already present in the preceding discourse, or in the general context of the utterance). As well as the topic, we also have the 'comment', which is what is said about the topic. The comment corresponds to 'new' information – for example, the information that John (the topic) has been working hard all day (the comment).

Some languages (such as Japanese) explicitly mark the topic of the sentence with a special particle. Other languages (such as English) have other ways of marking topics. One of these ways is 'topicalisation', where a constituent is turned into the topic of the sentence by being moved to the front (as in *'John I cannot stand'* instead of *'I cannot stand John'*). Topics are usually unstressed and occur early in the sentence. It is important not to confuse topic with the somewhat similar notion of the 'focus' of a sentence (which is usually stressed). Some linguists also use the term 'discourse topic', which is the vaguer notion of what a piece of discourse is about.

see also...

Discourse; Focus; Stress

Transformational–generative grammar

Traditional grammars provide some information about a language, but this information is incomplete and is stated in an informal way. Noam Chomsky revolutionised linguistics in the 1950s by proposing that the goal of linguistics should be to develop grammars that give a complete description of what knowledge a native speaker of that language must have. This description should consist of a set of rules that could be used to generate any grammatical sentence of the language (and no ungrammatical sentence): in theory, a computer programmed with these rules would be able to distinguish grammatical sentences of the language from ungrammatical sentences. Chomsky called such a grammar 'generative'.

There are many different kinds of generative grammar depending on what kind of rules are used. Chomsky himself argued for one particular kind of generative grammar he called a 'transformational grammar'. Transformational grammars have two kinds of rules: those which specify how words should be combined to form sentences or phrases ('phrase-structure rules'), and those which specify how sentences of one type can be converted into sentences of a different type. For example, phrase-structure rules would construct the sentence *'Teresa hit the ball'*, but the related sentence *'The ball was hit by Teresa'* would be constructed from the first sentence by applying a transformational rule (in this case, the rule for passives).

Chomsky showed that a transformational grammar was far more efficient, since many sentences could be formed from other sentences using transformational rules. This not only made the phrase-structure rules more simple, but captured the fact that certain sentences (such as actives and passives) seem to be related to each other.

see also...

Chomsky; Deep and surface structure; Tree diagram; Voice

Tree diagram

The grammar of a language tells us how words are combined to form phrases and how phrases are combined to form sentences. This structure can be represented in the form of a 'tree diagram' (also known as a 'tree structure' or 'phrase marker'). For example, the structure of the sentence *'John likes ripe mangoes'* might be represented as follows:

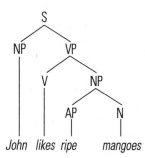

This (simplified) tree diagram indicates that the sentence (S) is made up of a noun phrase (NP) and a verb phrase (VP), that the verb phrase is itself made up of a verb (V) and a noun phrase, and so on. Tree diagrams show how a sentence can be constructed using the rules of the grammar. For example, the above tree could be constructed by rules such as:

S → NP VP; VP → V NP and so on (where '→' can be read as 'is made up of').

Any point in a tree where a branch starts or finishes is known as a 'node' (i.e. those points labelled S, VP, V, *likes* and so on in the tree opposite). A 'family' metaphor is used when discussing the relationship between nodes in a tree. A 'mother' node is connected by a branch in the tree to the 'daughter' node below it. (The mother is said to 'dominate' the daughter.) Two nodes which have the same mother are known as 'sisters'.

see also...

Chomsky; Phrase; Transformational–generative grammar

Typology

There are two main ways in which languages can be classified into groups. They can be classified in terms of their historical (or 'genetic') relationships, which is the subject matter of historical linguistics. Thus English, Latin, Hindi and Albanian would be classified together (along with many other languages), because they are all related historically. Languages can also be classified according to similarities in their structure. Thus English, Chinese and Thai might be classified together on the basis that they all have a subject–verb–object word order, although they are historically unrelated. Classifying languages on the basis of their structure is known as 'typology'.

If typological classifications of languages are to be useful, it is important that not just any structural feature be chosen as the basis of classification. For example, we could classify the world's languages according to whether they have the sound /w/, but the resulting typology would tell us nothing particularly interesting about principles governing language. Typologies are useful if they shed light on fundamental properties shared by languages (called 'universals'). For example, languages with verb–subject–object word order always have prepositions (other languages have 'postpositions', which follow nouns rather than preceding them). This suggests that there is some fundamental principle of language that governs both prepositions and basic word order (indeed, a syntactic principle to account for this has been proposed).

The most common typologies are those based on word order. Other common (though less useful) typologies are based on whether a language has tones, and whether it is analytic or synthetic.

see also...

Analytic and synthetic language; Tone language; Universal; Word order

Universal

Certain facts are true of all human languages and these are known as 'universals'. For example, every language has nouns and verbs, every language has sentences made up of phrases, and no language creates questions by reversing the order of words in the sentence. Facts that are true of most languages, but not all, are sometimes known as 'universal tendencies'. Universals are of great interest to linguists, since they provide us with vital information about the nature of language.

We must be cautious, however, as not all universals are the result of linguistic factors. For example, the fact that all languages have a word meaning 'water' is more likely to do with the universality of water than any fact about language itself. Many universals can also be explained by the fact that we all perceive the world in similar ways. For example, all languages divide up the colour spectrum in predictable ways, but this is due to the properties of our system of vision and nothing to do with language itself.

Those universals that are a result of genetically specified aspects of language are known as 'universal grammar'. Of particular interest are universals of the form 'if a language has x then it also has y' (e.g. if a language has verb–subject–object word order, then it will always have prepositions). These are known as 'implicational universals' and can provide evidence for more abstract properties of language.

see also...

Typology; Universal grammar

Universal grammar

A remarkable fact about the world's languages is how similar they are. You may be surprised by this: after all, to the casual observer (and the adult language learner!) there may seem to be very little at all in common between English and Zulu, say. But this appearance of diversity is something of a smokescreen created by certain superficial differences. All human languages are structured in remarkably similar ways. Another remarkable fact about language is the apparent ease and speed with which children acquire it. Most linguists believe that these facts provide evidence that we are born with certain properties of language hardwired into our brains: they do not need to be learned by children, which makes language acquisition easier, and they are shared by all humans, which explains their universality. These properties of language are known as 'universal grammar' or 'UG'.

UG can be seen as the template from which languages are constructed. It does not specify every property of language or there could be no differences between languages at all. Rather, it specifies some properties, offers a choice of values for others (e.g. word order) and does not specify other properties at all (e.g. what sound should be used to mean 'dog'). Not all universal properties of language are a result of UG, however. Some may be the result of other factors, such as the need for language to be usable. For example, no language has only two sounds. This may be because such a language would be almost unusable (imagine trying to create thousands of different words out of just the sounds /a/ and /b/!), and nothing to do with UG.

see also...

Acquisition of language; Creoles and pidgins; Universal

Utterance

onsider a sentence such as *'I live in London'*. This sentence is no doubt uttered many times every day. And each of these utterances will be different: some will be louder, some will be quieter, some will be faster, some will be said with a higher pitch and so forth. But every one of these utterances will be of the *same* English sentence. A sentence, then, is an abstract linguistic entity. Actual uses of a sentence are called 'utterances' of that sentence. (Sometimes, an utterance may not correspond to any sentence at all, for example if a speaker is interrupted part-way through a sentence and produces an utterance such as *'But I really think that…'*.)

Different utterances of a sentence can differ in their *meaning* as well. For example, the sentence *'I live in London'* means something different when it is spoken by different people: when I utter it, it means 'Richard Horsey lives in London' (which happens to be true); when uttered by Bill Clinton, it means 'Bill Clinton lives in London' (which happens to be false). Linguists therefore distinguish two kinds of meaning. 'Linguistic meaning' is the meaning a sentence has regardless of who utters it, or what situation it is uttered in. 'Speaker meaning', in contrast, is the meaning conveyed by the use of a sentence in a particular context. The branch of linguistics that looks at speaker meaning is known as 'pragmatics', while sentence meaning is studied in 'semantics'.

see also...

Deixis; Grice; Pragmatics; Semantics; Sentence

Verb

Words such as *go, finish* and *seem* are members of the class of verbs. They were defined in traditional grammars as expressing actions, but this definition is inaccurate, since many verbs (such as *seem*) do not express actions at all. Linguists prefer to define verbs (like other parts of speech) according to their grammatical properties.

Verbs can change their form to indicate tense (e.g. past, present), aspect (e.g. continuing action, completed action), mood (e.g. imperative), person and number. Not all languages make use of all these distinctions.

The verb is in some sense the most important element in a sentence, since it influences the choice of subject, object and other elements. Verbs may be classified according to the number of other elements they require to be in the sentence. For example, the verb *buy* requires a direct object (so we have *I bought a book*, but not **I bought*), but the verb *sleep* does not (we can say *I slept*). Verbs which require a direct object are known as 'transitive', and those which do not are known as 'intransitive'.

Many verbs have both a transitive and intransitive use (so we find *I ate* as well as *I ate dinner*). Verbs which take two objects are known as 'ditransitive' (e.g. *He gave me the book*).

Verbs may occur in groups (e.g. *He **will be finishing** soon*). The main verb (*finish*) is known as the 'lexical verb', and the others as 'auxiliaries'. When a verb is followed by a preposition to form a unit with a distinct meaning (such as *wake up*), this is referred to as a 'phrasal verb'.

see also...

Aspect; Mood and modality; Morphology; Part of speech; Tense

Voice

The sentences *'The dog bit the man'* and *'The man was bitten by the dog'* have approximately the same meaning, even though *the man* is the subject in one case and *the dog* is the subject in the other. The difference is one of 'voice'. Because the subject in the first sentence is in some sense the 'actor', we say that such sentences are in the 'active voice'. In the latter sentence, the subject is acted upon, hence 'passive', and we say that such sentences are in the 'passive voice'.

In general, we may say that voice is a grammatical property of the verb and expresses the way in which the subject (or object) is related to the meaning expressed by the verb. Changing the voice of a sentence does not affect the basic meaning of that sentence (i.e. 'who did what to whom'), although clearly it changes meaning in subtle ways. English only has active and passive voices, but other languages have further contrasts. For example, the 'middle voice' of Classical Greek is used when the subject is affected by its own action, and would be used in sentences such as *'I washed myself'* or *'He combed his hair'*. Some other

languages have a causative voice. In a causative sentence, the subject is whatever caused the action expressed by the verb.

Certain verbs do not occur in all voices. For example, English has verbs such as *have* and *cost* which do not occur in the passive (we cannot say * *'A cold is had by me'*), and also verbs such as *think* and *say*, which have passive uses that do not correspond to any active sentence (e.g. *'John was thought to be dead'* cannot be expressed as *'Someone thought John to be dead'*).

see also...

Grammatical category; Verb

Vowel

Speech sounds are divided into two categories: 'vowels' and 'consonants'. Vowels are defined as sounds made without significant narrowing of the vocal tract, allowing the air to escape evenly over the centre of the tongue. If the air escapes only through the mouth, a vowel is said to be 'oral'. If some air also escapes through the nose, a vowel is said to be 'nasal'. English does not make use of nasal vowels, although they are common in many languages (e.g. in French, in words such as *fin* 'end').

In addition to 'oral' and 'nasal', vowels are also classified according to the position of the tongue in the mouth. Two things are important: tongue height ('high', 'mid' or 'low') and tongue fronting ('front', 'central' or 'back'). Try repeating the sounds [a] and [i] in sequence, and notice how your tongue moves up and down as you do so. This is because [a] is a low vowel, and [i] is a high vowel.

Other features used to classify vowels include: whether the lips are rounded (as in [o] or [u]) or unrounded (as in [a] or [e]), their duration ('long' or 'short'), whether they are tense or lax and the tone of the vowel. In some vowels, the tongue does not remain still, but moves from one place in the mouth to another. These vowels are known as 'diphthongs' (e.g. the '*ai*' sound in *bait*).

see also...

Consonant; Tone and tone language

Word

Providing a definition of what a word is might seem trivial – after all, surely words are those things we write with space between them. But in fact it is not always easy to define words in this way. First, many languages (such as most in India) do not put spaces between words when they write. Second, there are many languages that do not have a written form and speech does not have 'gaps' like written words do (just try listening to a language you don't understand and decide where each word ends!).

Even in languages like English, which do write words with spaces between them, there can be difficulties: is *lawn mower* two words, or is it only one word (*lawnmower*)? One of the reasons it is difficult to define 'word' is that we use the term to mean several different things. Linguists distinguish between these different uses. An 'orthographic word' is the thing we write with a space at either end. A 'phonological word' is something pronounced as a single unit, identified by phonological criteria. 'Lexical items' or 'lexemes' are those items which are listed in dictionaries as separate words, and (more importantly for linguists) are stored mentally as individual items. Thus *mow, mows, mowing* and *mowed* would all be considered the same lexical item, *mow*. An idiom such as *kick the bucket* would also be considered a single lexical item, because it must be listed separately along with its unpredictable meaning 'die'.

see also...

Lexicon

Word order

In English, we say *'Cat bites dog'*; in Burmese *'Cat-dog-bites'*; in Welsh *'Bites-cat-dog'*. Almost every language has a particular order in which it puts the words of a sentence. In some languages, this order is rigid. In others, word order may be virtually free, but there is usually still a 'default' or 'preferred' order. Word order is usually expressed in terms of three basic elements of sentences: subject (S), verb (V), and object (O). Thus English (along with French, Chinese, Thai) are all SVO; Burmese (along with Turkish and Japanese) are SOV; and Welsh (as well as Tongan and some forms of Arabic) are VSO.

The other three possible orders, VOS, OVS and OSV are either extremely rare or non-existent. Note that in each of these the object precedes the subject, so there appears to be a strong preference in language for the subject to precede the object.

Which word order a language has also determines many other of its properties. For example, all VSO languages have prepositions (rather than postpositions). The great majority of OSV languages place relative clauses before the noun they modify (unlike English, where in a relative clause construction such as *the book that I wrote*, the relative clause *that I wrote* follows the noun *book*). There are many other similarities among languages with the same word order. These similarities suggest that there are important principles of language that govern many aspects of the order of words in a sentence.

see also...

Typology

Writing system

The ability to speak is a part of human biology. It comes as naturally to us as building nests does to birds. We have had the ability to speak for tens of thousands of years, but the first writing systems were developed only around 5000 years ago. Even today, many people go through their lives without ever learning to read or write, but cases of people who never learn a language are truly rare. It seems, then, that language and writing are fundamentally different: whereas writing is a human invention, language is a biologically evolved ability.

Before humans invented writing systems, they used written symbols for specific tasks, such as trade and taxation. A true writing system, however, allows any utterance of the language to be written down. It is not known who invented the first such system, but it is likely that writing systems were developed in several different parts of the world independently.

There are three main types of writing system. In one type, each morpheme of the language is represented with a different symbol. The earliest know systems were of this type and such a system is still in use for Chinese. Most writing systems in use today represent sounds rather than morphemes. For example, the Japanese *kana* scripts use a different symbol to represent each syllable (such as /ka/, /ku/ or /wa/). This type of system works best for languages with a fairly small number of different syllables. The last kind of system is the most common: alphabetic writing. These systems (such as English) use symbols to represent individual sounds. This makes them relatively simple, since the number of different sounds in a language is fairly small.

see also...

Morpheme; Syllable; Word

Further reading

If you would like to learn more about linguistics, you may find the following books useful:

Aitchison, J. (1999) *Teach Yourself Linguistics*, 5th edition. London: Hodder & Stoughton.
Aitchison, J. (1998) *The Articulate Mammal*, 4th edition. London: Routledge.
Fromkin, V. & Rodman, R. (1998) *An Introduction to Language*, 6th edition. New York: Harcourt Brace Jovanovich.
Pinker, S. (1994) *The Language Instinct*. London: Penguin.
Smith, N.V. (1999) *Noam Chomsky: Ideas and Ideals*. Cambridge: Cambridge University Press.

Also available in the series